'TONGUE' TRAP

Dr. D. K. Olukoya

THE

TONGUE TRAP

Dr. D. K. Olukoya

The Tongue Trap

1st Printing - August, 1999

ISBN 978-2947-70-9

322, Herbert Macaulay Way,
Yaba P 0 Box 12272, Ikeja, Lagos
 Website www.battlecryng com
email, sales@battlecryng.com
Phone 2348033044239,01-8044415

I salute my wonderful wife, Pastor Shade, for her invaluable support in the ministry.

I appreciate her unquantifiable support in the book ministry as the cover designer, art editor and art adviser
All Scripture quotation is from the King James Version of the Bible

OTHER BOOKS BY DR. D. K. OLUKOYA

* Prayer and Fasting booklet in English, French, Hausa, Igbo and Yoruba languages

CONTENTS

1

The tongue trap

The women fellowship of a very large church invited me to one of the most well attended programmes in the history of that church.

The women embarked on a massive publicity drive and invited several men and women. The women were so excited about the programme that they put their best into the planning. Most of them succeeded in getting their husbands to attend the programme. Although most of those husbands were extremely busy executives who had no time for the church, yet, they came in large numbers. The women felt that the opportunity of having me as the guest speaker was going to be used by God to usher peace into homes which were at the verge of collapse.

True to their expectations, God brought signs and wonders and transformed several homes through the instrumentality of the word of God and warfare prayers. However, God brought out lots of startling revelations concerning the lives of the women who attended the programme. About a dozen women came to see me for personal prayer and counselling. They felt that they needed more help in spite of the fact that we had spent a quality time doing aggressive warfare for the peace, stability and progress of the homes which were represented in that congregation. I decided to give them more personal help since they appeared desperate concerning their needs.

The first woman came in and spent a long time complaining about her husband and her undesirable home condition. However, I did not only listen to her I also took time to listen to the voice of the Holy Spirit. I waited patiently for her to finish her long story. What the Lord told me ran contrary to what she was saying.

The Holy Spirit told me that the woman was caged by her mouth. I told her that I understood what she said. I told her "Madam your problem is a very simple one. Your problems will be solved immediately you run your mouth through a session of deliverance." "I don't understand what you are saying," she said. I called one of my assistants and asked him to explain further to her.

The second woman came in and spent a long time expressing what she felt was her problem to me. As usual, I listened to her long winding story. The Holy Spirit also told me that the problem of the second woman was her tongue.

The case of the third woman was the most pathetic. Again, her problem bordered on her home. The Lord opened my eyes when I was praying for her. There was a hole at the centre of her lips and a rope was attached to it. The long rope was used to pull her by a terrible looking giant. After praying I told her, "A wicked strongman is after your life. However, the strongman is succeeding because of your wrong use of your mouth."

At the end of that counseling section, I discovered that most of the women had brought problems into their homes through careless use of their tongues.

THE POWER OF THE TONGUE

The Bible says in

> **Prov. 18.7: A fool's mouth is his destruction, and his lips are the snare of his soul.**

This passage shows us that the mouth can be destructive. The lips can also become a trap, which will not only catch the body but will also catch the soul. The Bible concludes that all those who do not know how to make use of their mouths are fools.

The psalmist knows the type of awesome power that resides in the tongue. That is why he prayed, "Set a watch O Lord before my mouth. Keep the door of my lips" (Psalm 141: 3). The psalmist called upon God to set a watch over his tongue because he knew that the tongue is capable of causing great damage if it is allowed to run loose.

What lesson can we learn from these Bible passages?

1. A discussion is an exchange of knowledge while an argument is an exchange of ignorance. It becomes clear, therefore, that people will achieve more positive results in life, if they do more of discussion than argument. If you remove argument from the home, more than half of family problems will be over.

2. The voice of silence is the loudest. There are times when you get your best result by keeping quiet. There was a particular man in the Bible, who did not want to keep his mouth shut. Zechariah would have achieved wonderful results if he had kept quiet. His speech made the angel to tell him that he was going to be dumb for a season. Zechariah lost his speech and had to use his hand to gesticulate. Therefore, silence does not make you foolish. Silence sometimes makes you wise. Remember the Bible says, "A fool's mouth is his own destruction."

3. Your ears function better when your mouth is shut. If you are going to spend your time talking all the time, you will not be able to hear what others are saying.

4. Wisdom is saying nothing when there is nothing to say. It is not compulsory that you must always have something to say. You don't have to pass comment on everything that happens around you. I came across two middle-aged women when I was a student several years ago. The two women ran their mouth loose on everything they saw in the street. They abused everyone who came across their way. They passed sarcastic comments on everyone; either the people were friends or total strangers.

5. You are no longer a controller of words once the words are spoken. Once a statement is uttered, you no longer have any control over it. The Bible says, "Life and death are in the power of the tongue."

6. *He who gossips to you will gossip about you.*

7. *He who speaks is sowing, he who listens is reaping.* This shows that it is better to listen than to speak.

8. *A wise person talks less and thinks more. He does not waste his words.*

9. *An average person spends about one fifth of his lifetime talking.* Research has shown that an average man speaks some 25,000 words per day, while the average woman speaks some 50,000 words per day.

10. *Just as a reckless driver can cause terrible damage, a reckless tongue can also cause destruction.*

11. *Gossiping and lying go hand in hand.*

12. *If you say nothing, nobody will repeat it.*

13. *If you refuse to listen to gossip, no gossip will be spread.*

14. *The tongue can determine your spiritual health.* If you are sick spiritually, your tongue will betray the condition of your health

15. *What has taken you years to do can be destroyed by the tongue in a few seconds.*

16. *Many stories change for the worse when people keep on repeating them.*

17. *The tongue has caused us more trouble than*

any other organ in the body.

18.   *Your little tongue can kill or make alive.*
Why don't you say this to yourself, "My tongue will not kill me, in the name of Jesus."

The tongue has destroyed a lot of people. When last did you say something unkind to someone?

When last did you say something that turned put to be untrue of another person? When last did you run somebody down with what you said? When last did you regret something which you said?
When last did you help to spread gossip? When last did you engage in an angry outburst? When last did you exaggerate stories which you did not confirm?

When last did you use God's name in vain? When last did you wish that you have remained silent?
The bottom line of what I have said so far is that the tongue has trapped many people.

It is unfortunate that many people have been trapped through their tongues. If you try to stick out your tongue it will come out as a serpent.

Somebody asked an old sage, "Sir, what is the most risky thing in the world?" "The tongue," he said. He was asked the second question, "What is the most harmful thing in the world?" "The tongue", he said. The old man, around 100 years, must have talked out of a series of experience. He knew that the tongue is capable of doing the most terrible thing, as well as the most wonderful thing on earth.

MAJOR DEMONS OF THE TONGUE

The tongue can be very destructive and unless you learn how to control it, that little member of your body can set your life on fire. The tongue will be set on fire after it has succeeded in setting the entire body on fire. You must allow God to control your tongue.

There are some demons that make the human tongue their abode. These evil spirits have built mansions in the tongue.

The tongue has no respect for anybody. What then are the major demons of the tongue? I shall enumerate them.

Lying. Lying is one of the principal demons that operate in the human tongue. Lying has become so rampant today that many so-called Christians are now chief liars. It was not so in the good old days. Those days, whenever men and women were to be appointed to sensitive positions in banks and other important establishments, they normally approached church leaders to recommend trusted Christians to fill such positions. Today, the story has changed. The born again man is the first to lie, steal and cheat.

The kind of lies which some people tell today, are no longer ordinary ones. Listen to some people and you wil be sure that there is a demonic force behind the lies they tell.

Negative speech. Another activity of the satanic demon, which operates through the tongue, is negative speech. A lot of people today are addicted to speaking negative words. Such people do not say anything that is positive.

Boasting and bragging. Many people are allowing demonic spirits to oppress them by boasting and bragging.

Talkativeness. There are people today who can surpass parrots in talking. They are controlled by demon of talkativeness. The devil influences them to keep on talking even when there is no reason to say anything.

Being hasty in speech. There are people who do not think before they speak. Such people start giving you an answer before you finish asking your question. They are so hasty that it is clear that they are influenced by the power of hell.

Immorality. That is another demon of the tongue. Many peoples lips are filled with immoral words, They make all kinds of statements that dwell on immorality.

Using Gods name in vain. That is another area of demonic influence.

Slander. A lot of people utter false statements and give false reports about friends or neighbours. Their purpose is to destroy the reputation of the people hey are talking about.

Backbiting. Many people today speak evil against people in their absence. The Bible says, "In many things we offend all. If any man offend not in word, the same is a perfect man and also able to bridle the whole body" (James 3: 1). Therefore, ability to control your tongue is a sign of perfection.

Gossip. This is destructive. However, many people cherish it.

THE IRREPARABLE LOSS

Many people are fond of gossiping. A lot of people today are incurable gossips. The only time such people detest gossip is when other people are gossiping about them.

A young man went everywhere speaking against a man of God. He became sorry, later, for what he had done and decided to make amends. He approached the man of God and expressed regret over spreading gossip about him. The man of God said that he would surely forgive the young man. However, he told him that he had one assignment for him before pronouncing total forgiveness. The young man became excited and told the man of God that he was ready to comply with whatever he would be told to do.

The man of God instructed him to get some feathers and go from door to door, placing a feather at each door step until the entire community was covered.

The young man was eager to receive complete forgiveness from the man of God. He ran to get some feathers and spent days adorning doorsteps with feathers of various colours and sizes. He ran back to the man of God and said, Sir, Ive finished the assignment. Can I now receive your forgiveness? The man of God said, Wait a minute. Youve not finished carrying out my assignment. Now, go and bring all the feathers back to my house.

This young man became confused. He told the man of God that, that will not be possible. Sir, the wind would have blown off almost all the feathers. I dont think it is possible for anyone to gather the feathers again. Then the young man realised that the man of God was teaching him a lesson. He realised that just as it was impossible to gather the feathers, it is also impossible to correct all the wrong impression which you must have given people as a result of a gossip.

The evil seed that you sow when you gossip, the rumours you spread when talking about things that are not edifying, cannot be uprooted. It will grow into evil trees. It is impossible to undo the damage which is done when you allow yourself to be used by the devil to speak evil words.

THE CHARACTER OF THE GOSSIP

Who is a gossip? It is the person who goes around gossiping. The Bible teaches that you must go to your brother and settle a quarrel with him privately. If he fails to accept what you are saying, the Bible commands you to take another believer with you and go to him for further settlement. If he refuses further settlement you have another option. You can go ahead and take the case to the church. If he refuses to hear the church, the Bible still commands you to regard him as an unbeliever who needs prayer. The Bible does not give you any allowance to gossip about somebody who offends you.

Those who are misusing their tongues are heading towards hell fire. The Bible commands us, Thou shall not go up and down as a tail bearer among thy people (Lev. 19:16).

The Bible also tells us that God does not want any of His children to go about as a talebearer. The Bible says, "Whoso privily slandereth his neighbour, him will I cut off: him that hath an high look and a proud heart will not I suffer" (Psalm 101:5).

Gossip is for people who are not spiritually minded. It is for people who lack brotherly love those who hate others.

Gossip is for idle people. It is a vice which must not be found among Gods people.

This message is from the heart of God. Gossip has done untold damage in the church and in the world. Men and women have caused terrible damages through gossiping and backbiting.

Once the devil discovers that your tongue is loose, he will make use of it to introduce problems into your life. The problem of the tongue is so deadly, that all serious Christians must destroy its evil influence. You must tame your tongue and cultivate that habit of putting it to a positive use.

ESCAPING THE TONGUE TRAP

How then can we escape the tongue trap? Here are the steps.

Know the dangers inherent in the misuse of the tongue. The Bible makes it very clear that liars shall end up in hell fire. Gossips shall also end in hell fire. Lying, backbiting and slander will lead you to hell fire. It will be tragic, for you not to get to heaven simply because you cannot control one of the smallest members of your body. You must remember that the Bible states that death and life are in the power of the tongue.

I once read about a white woman who was always fond of saying "O, my poor legs," each time she woke up in the morning. That was what she kept on saying everyday. She eventually ended up with an attack of arthritis on those legs. She was the one who put a curse on herself with her own mouth.

When someone says, "I can't make it." This is the worst season of my life. "Everything around me has turned upside down." "I'm in a bundle of affliction." "I'm tired of myself," etc. Such a person is programming evil into his life through the spoken word.

Winston Churchill was one of the most popular Prime Ministers. He found himself in the midst of a group of people who were gossiping about him. They said "Winston Churchill is growing old. He has become senile. He should leave the place in order to give room to another person." Churchill allowed them to say all that they had in mind. Then, he turned to them and said "Did anyone tell you he is deaf?"

People allow their tongues to become loose as a result of anger. If you are loose with your tongue, God will not put secrets into your hands. A lot of people complain that they are not hearing from God. How can God speak to them when they are busy talking all the time?

Recognise that the misuse of the tongue is a problem of the heart. The Bible says,

> **Either make the tree good, and his fruit good; or else make the tree corrupt, and his fruit corrupt: for the tree is known by his fruit. O generation of vipers, how can ye, being evil, speak good things? for out of the abundance of the heart the mouth speaketh (Matt. 12:33 34).**

The problem of the misuse of the tongue can be traced to the heart.

Understand why God gave you a tongue. If you do not know the use of some equipment, you may end up misusing them. Why did God give you a tongue? He gave you a tongue so that you can use it to glorify His name. Your tongue should rejoice, give glory to God and communicate His love and power to men and women.

Confess your sins, receive cleansing and forgiveness. Settle every sin that borders on the misuse of the tongue.

Refuse to yield your tongue to the devil. Do not allow the devil to use your tongue to spread his evil propaganda.

Minister deliverance on your tongue. If your tongue keeps on putting you into trouble, call the fire of God upon it in order to purify it. Ask all the demons on your tongue to depart.

You must ask yourself the following questions before you open your mouth to say anything:

i   Is it true?
ii   Do I need to say it?
iii   Will it do any good to anybody if I say it?
iv   Will Jesus say it?
v   Is it helpful?
vi   Is it edifying?
vii   Is it kind?
viii   Is it necessary?

If the answers to these questions are no, then you must keep your mouth shut. If you take this as a rule of life you will not listen to any statement made by anyone if such a person is not ready to repeat what he has said in the presence of the affected person. If you listen to gossips or rumour, you will end up receiving the same judgement as the person who is responsible for spreading the rumour.

A GREAT LESSON

A pastor who arrived in his new station decided to teach people the greatest lessons of their lives by discouraging rumours and gossips. Incidentally, I had warned the pastor to refrain from those who spread gossip and rumours.

As soon as he landed in his new post, one of the members came to his counseling office with the intention of spreading some gossips. She said, "Pastor, I just come to share a very useful information with you. Do you know what sister 'A' has been doing to her husband?" She wanted to continue spreading the rumour when the pastor stopped her saying, "Let me ask you a question before you continue? How many times have you prayed for the sister?" The member could not answer. The pastor simply ordered her out of his office.

Another member came to see him with another brand of rumour and said, "Have you heard about what Brother B did?" Again the pastor did not allow him to go far before he said How many minutes have you spent praying for him? The person could not answer him. That was how the Pastor walked out the second man. A number of other members kept on coming to spread rumours and gossips. He kept on showing every one of them the exit door.

What do you think would have happened, if that Pastor had encouraged the members who came to spread rumours or gossips?

Do you listen to rumours and useless information? Do you speak evil words? Do you listen to words of those who gossip? If you are fond of speaking and listening to destructive words about other people you are committing murder.

Do you speak when you are supposed to keep quiet? Do you speak words, which will condemn you on the day of judgement?

You must repent today. It would be disastrous if you end up in hell fire because you cannot control your tongue.

How terrible will it be if when you approach the gate of life you were told, "Sorry, you cannot enter this place. Your tongue is dirty." You will have no one to blame if you allow yourself to be trapped by your tongue. You must repent before the Lord if you dont want your tongue to lead you to hell fire. You must go to God in prayer and tell Him that you are sorry for all the ungodly words, which you spoke to men and women.

PRAYER POINTS

1. I release myself form every cage of the tongue, in the name of Jesus.

2. My tongue will not send me to hell fire, in the name of Jesus.

3. Holy Spirit, control my tongue, in the name of Jesus.

4. I reverse every curse that I issued upon my own life with my own tongue, in the name of Jesus.

5. O Lord, let my tongue bring forth life.

6. Everything deposited against me in the ground, be roasted, in the name of Jesus.

7. I dismantle every covenant of poverty, in the name of Jesus.

8. I am rising up, no power shall pull me down, in the name of Jesus. (Pray this prayer point with all you heart.)

9. O Lord, rearrange failure out of my life.

10. Every power holding evil meetings against me, O God, arise and scatter them, in the name of Jesus.

2

Tongue under Bondage

The tongue is one of the most powerful parts of the body, which is capable of doing much good or much evil.

Mark 7:35 describes clearly the power of the tongue:

And straightway his ears were opened, and the string of his tongue was loosed, and he spake plain.

God has deposited lots of powers and ability into the lives of men and women. Some of the most important powers include the power of imagination, power of creativity, power of responsibility, power to labour and get rewards, power to exercise dominion, power to subdue other creatures, power to pursue and overtake enemies and recover what they stole from you, power to pull down and root out all evil things and build good things.

These are examples of the type of power which God has given to man.

When Jesus came on the scene he began to give power to teach, to heal, to witness and to deliver men and women. Jesus specifically stated that he came to give us power to do greater things than He did. However, all the power which is given by God to mankind is tied to the spoken word.

These powers become effective when you begin to speak out through your mouth. That is why most of the problems which men and women have today can be traced to the fact that their tongues are under bondage.

THE SATANIC WEAPON

Many tongues are under bondage today. Apostle James highlights the importance of the tongue and shows us that if we are under bondage in the area of the tongue the totality of our lives are under bondage.

I want you to pay attention to the statements which James made through the inspiration of the Holy Spirit. We need to pay a particular attention, today, to the fact that the reason many peoples prayers are unanswered can be traced to the fact that the human tongue has been used by the devil to lead men and women into bondage.

> **James 1:26: If any man among you seem to be r religious, and bridleth not his tongue, but deceiveth his own heart, this man's religion is vain.**

The Bible teaches that all those who do not know how to control their tongues will end up with divine condemnation.
James further states:

> **My brethren, be not many masters, knowing that we shall receive the greater condemnation (James 3:1).**

This passage teaches that if you are able to control

your tongue, you will be able to control the whole of your body.

Let us read further from verse 3 to 12:

> Behold, we put bits in the horses' mouths, that they may obey us; and we turn about their whole body. Behold also the ships, which though they be so great, and are driven of fierce winds, yet are they turned about with a very small helm, whithersoever the governor listeth. Even so the tongue is a little member, and boasteth great things. Behold, how great a matter a little fire kindleth! And the tongue is a fire, a world of iniquity: so is the tongue among our members, that it defileth the whole body, and setteth on fire the course of nature; and it is set on fire of hell. For every kind of beasts, and of birds, and of serpents, and of things in the sea, is tamed, and hath been tamed of mankind: But the tongue can no man tame; it is an unruly evil, full of deadly poison. Therewith bless we God, even the Father; and therewith curse we men, which are made after the similitude of God. Out of the same mouth proceedeth blessing and cursing. My brethren, these things ought not so to be. Doth a fountain send forth at the same place sweet water and bitter? Can the fig tree, my brethren, bear olive berries? either a vine, figs? so can no fountain both yield salt water and fresh.

Although the tongue is a tiny member, it can start a very big flame.

The tongue has destroyed many families, wrecked companies, destroyed nations and brought communities into utter desolation.

The tongue is the most dangerous member of the human body.

Perhaps, God knew the danger inherent in the human tongue, that is why He gave you two eyes, two nostrils, two ears and one mouth. Nobody will desire to have two mouths because of the power of the single tongue, which he has in his mouth. Im sure you already know that you have more than enough problems with the single mouth which God has given to you. I wonder what will happen if you begin to have two tongues.

A PASSPORT TO HELL

Your tongue can be used to serve God and it can also be used to serve the devil.

The tongue is a very effective passport to hell fire. If you cannot control your tongue, it will control you. Many lives would have become wonderful and glorious if at a particular stage in their lives they became dumb like prophet Zechariah.

If the problem of the tongue could be removed from the lives of men and women, such lives would become wonderful beyond comparism.

When your tongue is under the control of God you will speak godly words. However, if your tongue is under the control of the devil you will speak satanic words.

Human lives are shaped and controlled by the tongue.

What you are going through in your life today is as a result of the kind of words you spoke previously. That is why God created seven openings in the human body and restricted the seventh one to a single opening and it has caused more problems than all the other openings put together.

The tongue can control circumstances surrounding every human being.

The children of the devil who practice black magic depend on the tongue to carry out their activities. That explains why they do not joke about the power of the tongue. A lot of Christians are killing themselves daily with their tongue.

The Bible says,

> Come, ye children, hearken unto me: I will teach you the fear of the LORD. What man is he that desireth life, and loveth many days, that he may see good? Keep thy tongue from evil, and thy lips from speaking guile (Psalm 34:11-13).

The fear of the Lord is demonstrated by exercising restraint and control over the tongue. In other words, the fear of the Lord starts from the tongue. Once you exercise control over your mouth, you are assured of the fact that you will see good days.

Prov. 13:3 says,

> He that keepeth his mouth keepeth his life: but he that openeth wide his lips shall have destruction.

A lot of people's lives are as if they are ignorant of this passage. Such people open their mouth wide and utter anything that comes to their mind.

The book of Proverbs has a lot to say about the problems of the tongue. Again it says,

> **Whoso keepeth his mouth and his tongue keepeth his soul from troubles (Prov 21:23).**

Exactly the same thing is said in Proverbs 15:14:

> **The heart of him that hath understanding seeketh knowledge: but the mouth of fools feedeth on foolishness.**

This passage reveals that the most dangerous activity anyone can get into is to indulge in using the mouth wrongly.

The most powerful commentary on the subject of the tongue can be found in Proverbs 18:21.
Death and life are in the power of the tongue: and they that love it shall eat the fruit thereof.

Many people are in the dark today concerning the mystery of the tongue. The totality of your life rises or falls on your tongue. That is why it is important for your tongue to come under the control of the Holy Spirit. Since the tongue is capable of controlling other members of the body you must ensure it is placed under divine control. This explains why the believer begins to speak in tongues when the Holy Ghost comes upon him.

If God can control your life through your tongue, you

will begin to please God. If God is unable to control your tongue, your life will become a bundle of sin and confusion. One secret which you ought to know is this: what you say with your tongue will eventually happen to you sooner or later. If you say bad things against yourself, your entire body will record it. It will come into manifestation sooner or later.

The question you ought to answer, therefore, is "Is my tongue under bondage?"

HOW TO RECOGNIZE THE TONGUE UNDER BONDAGE

It is very easy to know whether your tongue is under bondage. You must watch certain signals.

Excessive talking. If you come across someone who speaks 200 words per minute such a person has a great problem.

If you came across a group of people and only one of them overshadows all others through her voice such a person needs the deliverance of the tongue.

The Bible says,

In the multitude of words there wanteth not sin: but he that refraineth his lips is wise (Prov 10:19).
If you are superfluous in your speech you have a serious problem to solve.

Idle or careless words. Your tongue is under

bondage if you speak idle or careless words. If you spend your time gossiping and backbiting, you are under demonic influence.

Have you become a broadcasting officer for the devil? The Bible says,

> **Thou shalt not go up and down as a talebearer among thy people: . . . (Lev 19:16).**

Those who gossip are doing the devil's work.

Lying. Some people are experts in lying. It is strange that Christians also tell lies. A lying tongue needs deliverance.

Being hasty in speech. A lot of people operate as if they were driven by a demonic force. They are quick to speak and slow to hear.

The Bible says,
> **They angered him also at the waters of strife, so that it went ill with Moses for their sakes: Because they provoked his spirit, so that he spake unadvisedly with his lips (Ps 106:32 -33).**

Do you speak unadvisedly like Moses? Are you hasty to make ungodly statement?

Swearing and cursing. This is an evidence of the presence of demonic powers at the tip of your tongue. The Bible says

> **But I say unto you, Swear not at all; neither by heaven; for it is God's throne: Nor by the earth; for**

it is his footstool: neither by Jerusalem; for it is the city of the great King. Neither shalt thou swear by thy head, because thou canst not make one hair white or black (Matt 5:34-36).

The apostle Peter also tells us,

For he that will love life, and see good days, let him refrain his tongue from evil, and his lips that they speak no guile: (1 Pet 3:10).

Many believers speak the language of hell today. If you use abusive language on human beings created by God you are demonstrating the fact that your tongue is under satanic influence. Some people curse themselves whenever anything happens to them. Such people are under some evil influence.

DEMONIC INFLUENCE

Through chanting of incantations. Let me make this important statement. If your parent taught you how to chant incantations before you gave your life to Christ, you need to go through the deliverance of the tongue. You must allow the fire of the Holy Spirit to neutralise the effect of the evil incantations. Those incantations made you to invoke powers of darkness. Your life cannot be freed from demonic influence if you fail to remove the effect of such deadly incantations from your life.

Through negative recitation of the book of Psalms. You also have a lot of work to do if you used to recite the book of Psalms. They tell people to recite a particular psalm seven times and call the name of the counterfeit angels 21 times. This is a sign of being under bondage. The Bible does not ask anyone to pray in the name of any angel.

Through singing the praise of idols. If you used your tongue to sing the praise of idols before you became born-again, you must run yourself through serious deliverance. That is why such people generally find it difficult to receive baptism of the Holy Spirit. When we minister the Holy Ghost to some people and they are encouraged to speak in tongues such people say "I cant. My tongue is heavy." That is an evidence of being under bondage.

Through oral sex. Some people have invited demons into their lives by going into oral sex. Demons easily come into the lives of men and women who indulge in oral sex.

Through drinking of strange drinks. Others have put their tongues under bondage, by drinking strange local herbs or the so-called holy water from white garment churches. Sharing ritual drinks with others during demonic meetings also leads to bondage. Licking charms, eating 'holy' salt and sharing cigarettes will also lead to bondage.

Through speaking of foolish things. You speak foolish things and tell lies as if lying has been programmed into your life. Some people are ashamed to witness to others about Christ. They always talk about the negative side of things. They don't say anything positive. When people who have problems come to them, they increase the problem of their tongues.

Some people stammer when they were not born that way. Others were not born with the tendency to exaggerate but they begin to exaggerate because they are under demonic influence.

SOLUTION

What then is the solution to the problem of the bondage of the tongue?

Your tongue needs healing and deliverance. Some people are under compulsive evil habits because their tongues are under bondage. A deliverance minister may have to lay his hand on the tongue of this category of people.

Confession. You must recognise your spiritual need and be ready to accept the fact that you need deliverance. Even if you are a minister or a respected Christian worker, be truthful with yourself. One of the basic facts of your existence is that you will obtain what you confess with your mouth. If you speak negative words to yourself you will get negative result. You cannot create positive things.

If you talk positively all the time, you will always be surrounded by good things.

POSITIVE / NEGATIVE STATEMENTS

How then can you begin to use your tongue positively? What does your attitude to life look like? Are you fond of making negative statements like "I'm sick". "My life is filled with troubles." "I have lots of problems? " Such negative statements must give way to positive ones. But if you continue to make negative statements you will end up multiplying your problems.

Some of our ministers went to minister somewhere in Nigeria. A woman came requesting for help from them. They began to pray for her. All of a sudden, they discovered that she was not closing her eyes. They told her to close her eyes. She said, "Pastor, my situation is beyond prayer." That woman did not know the implication of what she was saying.

Others refuse to exercise faith in God when someone prays with them. They say, "I appreciate the fact that you have prayed for me. However, I want the strongest person here to pray for me. Any other prayer wont work." Such people are making a negative confession. If you continue to talk that way, the devil will continue to make your problems to be resistant to prayer.

Why don't you begin from now to think positively about everything around you? Think positively about your business, your future and everything around you. Instead of complaining, begin to say "It is well." "All things shall work together for my good." "I shall make it." "I have nothing to do with failure." Begin to practise speaking positive words about yourself and your situation for the next seven days and you will end up with lots of testimonies.

It is easy for people to give up whenever the devil challenges their prayers. Instead of saying, "I have been to that church and nothing seemed to have changed in my life," you must give verbal expression to your faith if you want it to bring results. Don't keep what you believe in your heart, speak it out. Boldly confess what you believe in your spirit for the devil and fellow human beings to hear.

Positive confession is an important part of the Christian life. There are three main things, which the believer can confess:

1. You can confess what the Lord has done in your life.
2. You can confess what the Lord is doing for you.
3. You can confess what the Lord is going to do for you.

The Lord has done a lot of things in your life. He has made you a new creature. He has sanctified you. He has given you the baptism of the Holy Spirit. You must confess all these.
The Bible says,

Say ye to the righteous, that it shall be well with him: for they shall eat the fruit of their doings (Isa 3:10).

Confess the word of the Lord and disregard whatever any prophet says to you if his prophecy runs contrary to the word of God.

The Bible says,

For I know the thoughts that I think toward you, saith the LORD, thoughts of peace, and not of evil, to give you an expected end (Jer 29:11).

Therefore, you must make use of your tongue in a positive way. Declare what God is saying about you with your lips.

Do not help the devil to broadcast what he is saying to you. Do not agree with symptoms of sicknesses which you are feeling in your body. Do not help the devil to broadcast what he is saying to you. Do not help human beings to broadcast their evil desires concerning your life. Keep saying what the Lord has said about you.

There is a very interesting story. Jerome was one of the most respected pioneers of the Christian faith who lived in one of the earliest centuries of church history. He was so vehement in his denunciation of false doctrine that he attracted a lot of hatred towards himself.

Jerome took ill and lay on a sick bed for a very long time. The enemies, those who were teaching false doctrines, began to rejoice thinking that he was going to die. They sent a delegate to him asking him to reconsider his stand. They even mocked him, saying that those of them who were labelled as teachers of false doctrine were not attacked by that type of sickness. They spent a long time deriding and mocking him. Jerome allowed them to say everything they had in their minds. When it appeared that they had concluded their funny statements, he gathered all his strength and roared with a loud voice: "I shall not die but live to declare the works of God." The heretics ran out of his room.

POSITIVE CONFESSION

The psalmist says, "I believe therefore have I spoken." *You must verbalise your faith.*

The woman with the issue of blood got her miracle through her confession for she said, "If I touch the helm of his garment I shall be made whole." She took a step of faith and she became healed. Jesus immediately felt that someone had drawn healing virtue out of Him. Jesus told her "Thy faith has made thee whole."

You must maintain what God has said about you. Untimely death is contrary to God's plan for your life. You have to confess this. You cannot become a victim of satanic attack unless you allow the enemy to catch you through sin.

Confession brings possession. Negative confession and silence will bring trouble. There are people who avoid aggressive prayer. Such people prefer silent prayer. They specialise in prayers that cannot affect the devil. Aggressive prayer is the only form of prayer that can move the mountains of your life away.

The Bible says,

I am the LORD thy God, which brought thee out of the land of Egypt: open thy mouth wide, and I will fill it (Ps 81:10).

People who think they are praying quietly, are only busy meditating upon their problems. Open your mouth wide and pray aggressively. Do not allow your thoughts to determine what your mouth says.

This reminds me of what we used to do when I was in the primary school many years ago. The first 30 minutes which we spent in the class, was always the hottest. If we stood up to greet our teachers in a sluggish manner by saying, "Good morning . . . s . . . i . .r," the teacher would ask us to remain on our feet and close our eyes. He would ask us to recite the multiplication table. Then, we would start in a chorus like this "2 x 1=2, 2 x 2=4, 2 x 3=6 . . .." The teacher would walk round the classroom with his cane in his hand. If you miss it the cane would land on your body, and you would be brought out for other punishments.

The manner with which our teacher handled us compelled almost everyone of us to master the multiplication table. Most students would behave unresponsively if teachers are not strict with them.

If God wants you to develop yourself and you refuse, He will resort to the use of disciplinary measures to force you to conform to the divine shape. If you don't want to learn certain things when the situation is very simple, God will make you to learn them in very tough circumstances.

The practice of consistently making the right confessions is both effective and powerful. You must maintain your confession even if what your senses were telling you seemed to run contrary to what God is saying to you.

If you need healing from God, you must disregard what the symptoms of the sickness are saying and hold on to the word of God.

What do you do if you have financial needs? You must confess the word of God. You must tell yourself, "My God shall supply all my needs according to His riches in Christ Jesus."

If the devil is trying to plague your heart with fear, you must tell yourself: "God has not given me the spirit of fear but of love, of power and of a sound mind.

The Bible says,

Let us hold fast the profession of our faith without wavering; (for he is faithful that promised;) (Heb 10:23).

A lot of things will try to shake you up, but you must

hold on to your faith. Victory is sure, provided you are able to hold on to your confession. Your tongue cannot be under bondage as long as you keep on confessing the word of God.

The tongue needs to be changed. The only thing that can tame the tongue is the word of God. That is why the Bible says,

> This book of the law shall not depart out of thy mouth; but thou shalt meditate therein day and night, that thou mayest observe to do according to all that is written therein: for then thou shalt make thy way prosperous, and then thou shalt have good success (Josh 1:8).

Do not allow the word of God to depart from your mouth. If you talk about problems, your life will be filled with difficulties. If you talk about sickness you will get sick. If you talk about poverty you will be poor. If you confess fear, you will continue to experience problems and failure.

FREEDOM FROM BONDAGE

Finally, you must remember that your tongue can bring you into the best condition in life and it can also bring you into the worst condition in life.

The Bible says,

> Death and life are in the power of the tongue: and they that love it shall eat the fruit thereof (Prov 18:21).

Again the Bible says,

Thou art snared with the words of thy mouth, thou art taken with the words of thy mouth (Prov 6:2).

This passage shows that the word of your mouth can be taken and used as a trap against you. If your tongue has been trapped, you must seek freedom today.

You must also go ahead to ask the Lord to enable you to tame your tongue. Do not forget that what you are going through today came into your life as a result of what you have been saying to yourself. If you want to experience dramatic changes in your life, you must align your words with the word of God.

The Bible says,

But what saith it? The word is nigh thee, even in thy mouth, and in thy heart: that is, the word of faith, which we preach; That if thou shalt confess with thy mouth the Lord Jesus, and shalt believe in thine heart that God hath raised him from the dead, thou shalt be saved (Rom 10:8-9).

What I want to say at this point is that just as you got yourself into bondage through your tongue, you must also go ahead to lead yourself into freedom and deliverance through your tongue.

You must cancel all the negative things which you have said about your life. Remember that no situation is beyond repair, if you can make use of your tongue in a positive manner. Nobody can say that you are finished when you decide to make use of the power of the tongue positively.

I may not know what you are going through right now but I am sure of the fact that your tongue can take you out of the worst situation into the best situation.

You can speak and move from poverty to prosperity, from trouble to peace, from sickness to health, from failure to success, from weakness to strength and from the valley to the mountain top.

Cultivate the habit of speaking positive words. Verbalise the conditions which you desire in your heart Change your life through the word of God.   Set your tongue free from all kinds of bondage. Say bye bye to physical and spiritual bondage. Let God set your tongue free. Don't allow the devil to change your tongue into a weapon of destruction. Surrender your tongue to God Let Him convert it into a mighty instrument for your utmost good and for the advancement of His kingdom on earth.

PRAYER POINTS

1. Father Lord, let Your anointing fall upon me now, in the name of Jesus.

2. You negative high places, that my tongue has built, I command you to be destroyed, in the name of Jesus.

3. Father, in the name of Jesus, go back to the time

that I started using my tongue and let every negative high place I have built with it be destroyed by fire.

4. Father, in the name of Jesus, loose my tongue from every bondage.

5. Father, in the name of Jesus, I withdraw all the negative confessions that I have made with my mouth.

6. Every dry bone of blessings in my life, I command you to loose your hold, in the name of Jesus.

7. Father, in the name of Jesus, promote my affairs from miracles to wonders.

3

Forces of self-destruction

You will agree with me that it is easier to destroy than to build. The Bible says:

The thief cometh not, but for to steal, and to kill, and to destroy: I am come that they might have life, and that they might have it more abundantly (John 10:10).

That devil is a destroyer. He releases the forces of destruction upon men, women and children.

A lot of people destroy themselves by receiving the spirit of destruction from the devil. Jesus knew that the devil had released the spirit of destruction into the world. That was why He came to destroy such wicked forces. The Bible says:

He that committeth sin is of the devil; for the devil sinneth from the beginning. For this purpose the Son of God was manifested, that he might destroy the works of the devil (I Jn 3:8).

The word of God tells us that Jesus came to destroy the works of the devil.

When the spirit of destruction is sent against a person, that spirit can destroy a number of things.

Some destructive spirits attack the human mind. Those who suffer from the problems initiated by the forces of destruction can be led into confusion and outright madness. The mind will be so confused that the victim will not know what he is doing. When somebodys mind is under bondage he will not be able to enjoy wholesomeness.

There is also the spirit of destruction of finances. This spirit leads to poverty, lack, debt, financial failure, leaking pockets and financial embarrassment. The spiritwill gradually destroy one's finances.

There is the spirit of body destruction. It destroys the body through sickness, mysterious diseases and all kinds of ailments.

There is the spirit of marriage destruction. This spirit leads to arguments, hatred, bad temper, fighting and separation or divorce. That is why three out of five marriages collapse.

We were told, sometime ago, that some witches gathered themselves together in South Africa and decided to fast for 200 days against Christian homes. Their purpose was to release the spirit of marriage destruction against Christian homes. These spirits are actually desperate; they do everything to carry out their activities.

The spirit of family destruction has also been released by the devil. That is why the spirit of death has continued to attack many families. There are some families where their members always die before they are 40 years old. We have had cases of families where up to five people are buried within one month. The spirit of family destruction is at work in such families.

This same spirit is responsible for accidents. I once witnessed a ghastly motor accident. A bus which was moving in front of our own vehicle suddenly somersaulted. You can imagine what happened to the people who were inside the bus. Here was a bus that was going smoothly without any problem. I actually saw the bus and I was surprised when I discovered that it tumbled within a very short time.

The spirit of family destruction also makes some men to get drunk until they can no longer find their way home. That is an evidence of the presence of the spirit of destruction in that person's life.

All these spirits are junior forces when compared with the spirit of self-destruction. The spirit of self-destruction makes people to be engaged in self-destructive activities. It is a wonder of all wonders that somebody could sit down, organise a battle against himself and begin to fight a war against himself.

A lot of people are actually fighting serious battles against themselves. Perhaps you have discovered that your life history has been punctuated by disappointments, frustrations, tragedy and many situations that have continued to baffle and confuse you.

The only explanation which can be given to the problems of self-destruction is that there are some invisible forces busy working, to determine ones destiny for good or for bad. If God could open your eyes to see the number of evil spirits which are working against the lives of men and women, you will be surprised. You will be more careful if God should give you a revelation of what is actually happening in the world.

A fact which many people know nothing about is that there are lots of dead people who are still living. There are multitudes of sick but active people. There are many enlightened men and women who are mad.

POWER OF SELF-DESTRUCTIVE FORCES

One of the greatest powers which is available in the whole universe is the power of words. Words can build and destroy. Words can create and pull down. If you are able to control your words you will control every other part of your body.

The devil is a fallen angel. He has no creative power. God did not give the power of creation to him. For the devil to do any evil or to create bad situations in the lives of men and women he has to rely on the power of words which was given to man. He has to influence a man to speak and manipulate the words to his own advantage. He has no creative power.

Self-destructive forces have led many people to impose curses upon themselves.

The forces of self-destruction are generally hidden. The words which you speak about yourself have frightening power that will actually scare you, if God would reveal to you how destructive the words are.

The Bible says:

But I say unto you, That every idle word that men shall speak, they shall give account thereof in the day of judgment. For by thy words thou shalt be

justified, and by thy words thou shalt be condemned (Matt 12:36 - 37).

Idle words

What are idle words? Idle words are words which are spoken carelessly, without meditation. If you allow your words to come out unchecked you have spoken an idle word. A lot of people speak some words without thinking about the effect they are likely to have on them and on others. Such words are idle or careless words. Jesus said that we should give an account of every idle word.

Therefore, if you speak 1,000 idle words, you will stand before the judgement seat of Christ and explain why you spoke them. Many of us joke with idle words. Do you know that the fact that you really did not mean what you said does not cancel the effect of such words, neither does it release you from accountability?

As far as the Bible is concerned all idle words carry weight. If you really face the standard of the Bible, you will discover that all the words which you speak are seriously taken by God. God has not given you any room to say what you do not mean, or what you dont want to account for. Once words are spoken, they are spoken. The next stage is accountability. That is why the Bible says:

Wherefore, my beloved brethren, let every man be swift to hear, slow to speak, slow to wrath: (James 1:19).

God expects us to be economical and thrifty with our

words. That is why he gave us two eyes, two ears, two nostrils but one mouth. The Bible says:

Thou art snared with the words of thy mouth, thou art taken with the words of thy mouth (Prov 6:2).

This is a serious matter. You can be trapped or snared by the words of your mouth. You must realise, today, that idle words are very costly. If you speak idle words you will face the consequences, sooner or later.

Marriage vows

Recently, I had some personal experiences which made me to ask the Lord some deep questions. I became concerned, as a minister, and I had to ask God some questions concerning Christian homes. I had to ask God why there are so many unstable homes and why there are so many partially married couples. I also asked the Lord to reveal to me the secret behind the problem of some sisters who are physically married but spiritually divorced.

The Lord gave me a shocker. He said, "Why don't you read through the traditional marriage vows? Why not examine the words which people pronounce during marriage ceremonies? Initially, what the Lord told me was not so clear in my spirit, I began to look for the type of marriage vows which people generally make on the day of their wedding. Let me give you an example.

"I brother X take you, sister Y, to be my wedded wife. To have and to hold, from this day forward, for better for worse, for richer and for poorer, in sickness and in health until death do us part."

Couples have made this pronouncement on themselves from time immemorial. People make such statements without knowing that they are speaking evil words which will affect their marriage sooner or later. True to their confessions, better and worse, sickness and health and richer and poorer, will mix together.

Instead of pronouncing, from the first day of their wedding, that they are going to stay together and expect sickness, worse conditions and poverty and making negative onfessions, why can't they pronounce positive words upon themselves? If you read such a vow on your marriage day, you must cancel, through prayer, every negative aspect of it. You can vow to stay with your spouse in health, for better and in prosperity.

You are not the only one who read that kind of vow. I also read it that way, several years ago. But thank God I have cancelled the negative word which was part of that traditional vow. No wonder, those who make up their minds saying that they will stay together for better or for worse are not finding it easy at all. Things are actually getting worse Those who said for richer or poorer are getting poorer, while those who said in sickness and in health are getting sick. In most cases, it is the woman that suffers.

Most couples have gotten what they read on their marriage day. God takes our words seriously. The devil also takes our words seriously. What the Lord spoke to me touched me. I went through the Bible but I did not find a single case of a Christian couple making that kind of pronouncement upon themselves. The devil is a legal expert. He uses our words to destroy us. You may deny your words and human beings may agree with you. However, you can be sure that God and the devil will still hold you responsible for what you denied.

Do you know that the words which you speak can remove your name from heaven's register? Let us take a look at a few examples:

PETER

> And as Peter was beneath in the palace, there cometh one of the maids of the high priest: And when she saw Peter warming himself, she looked upon him, and said, And thou also wast with Jesus of Nazareth. But he denied, saying, I know not, neither understand I what thou sayest. And he went out into the porch; and the cock crew. And a maid saw him again, and began to say to them that stood by, This is one of them. And he denied it again. And a little after, they that stood by said again to Peter, Surely thou art one of them: for thou art a Galilaean, and thy speech agreeth thereto. But he began to curse and to swear, saying, I know not this man of whom ye speak. And the second time the cock crew. And Peter called to mind the word that Jesus said unto him, Before the cock crow twice, thou shalt deny me thrice. And when he thought thereon, he wept (Mark 14:66 -72).

If you look at what Peter said and the manner with which he denied the Lord, you may think that he did not do anything which was seriously bad. I was shocked when I discovered that the fact that Peter denied being the Lord's disciple and went ahead to invoke curses upon himself made him to lose his position in heaven. I received a great shock of my life when I read the words of the angel in Mark 16:7:

> But go your way, tell his disciples and Peter that he goeth before you into Galilee: there shall ye see him, as he said unto you.

Peter was no longer reckoned with as one of the disciples. The angel instructed that the disciples of the Lord should be informed that the Lord has risen. Peter was singled ut as an ordinary person; not one of the Lords disciples. If Peter were to be on the right track, the angel would have said something like: "Tell all his disciples, including Peter, that the Lord is risen." By his own word, Peter forfeited his standing as a disciple. Thank God that Peter received mercy before it became too late.

It is on record that Peter denied Jesus three times. Each de ial was recorded in heaven and any of them could have hindered him from getting to heaven. Jesus had to help Peter by asking him three questions which made Peter to give three positive answers, thereby cancelling the three denials. Let us read the account in the gospel according to John:

> So when they had dined, Jesus saith to Simon Peter, Simon, son of Jonas, lovest thou me more than these? He saith unto him, Yea, Lord; thou knowest

that I love thee. He saith unto him, Feed my lambs. He saith to him again the second time, Simon, son of Jonas, lovest thou me? He saith unto him, Yea, Lord; thou knowest that I love thee. He saith unto him, Feed my sheep. He saith unto him the third time, Simon, son of Jonas, lovest thou me? Peter was grieved because he said unto him the third time, Lovest thou me? And he said unto him, Lord, thou knowest all things; thou knowest that I love thee. Jesus saith unto him, Feed my sheep (John 21:15 -17).

Peter was able to cancel the three denials which he had made. Thus he was able to break the self-imposed curses.

Freedom from the bondage of self-imposed evil words

The story of Peter's denial and the cancellation of the effect of the negative words which he spoke shows us the four steps which must be taken if any one wants to be released from the bondage which came into his life through bad confession.

Repentance - Peter repented. Peter wept bitterly when he realized that he had done the wrong thing. Therefore, the first stage is repentance.

Renouncement - Peter renounced his statements.

Cancellation - He cancelled the statements which he made previously.

Replacement - He replaced the negative statement with positive ones.

JACOB

Let us look at another example in the book of Genesis.

> My father peradventure will feel me, and I shall seem
> to him as a deceiver; and I shall bring a curse upon
> me, and not a blessing. And his mother said unto him,
> Upon me be thy curse, my son: only obey my voice,
> and go fetch me them (Gen 27:12 -13).

Jacob's mother prevailed upon him to deceive his father. Earlier on, Jacob was reluctant. However, he later succumbed to the pressure and accepted to carry out the evil plan. Jacobs mother, Rebecca, pronounced a curse upon herself, let us read verse 46:

> And Rebekah said to Isaac, I am weary of my life
> because of the daughters of Heth: if Jacob take a
> wife of the daughters of Heth, such as these which
> are of the daughters of the land, what good shall my
> life do me?

Rebekah later got tired of life and she eventually died as a result of a self-imposed curse.

The worst kind of destruction is self-destruction. It is very clear that some people are suffering from problems which were invited by them. Most of the problems which people go through today do not originate from God, the devil or human enemies, but are self-inflicted.

For example, if you open your mouth and say, "I am tired of living," you have succeeded in imposing a curse upon yourself. If you make negative remarks about yourself you are guilty of self-destruction.

If you say, "I am giving up. My situation will end up on a sad note", you are putting a curse on yourself. Those things may happen to you as specified by you.

Can you recall what happened when Jesus was crucified? Pilate told the people, "I found no fault in this man." They cried "Crucify him." Pilate said, But he has done nothing." Again they cried, "Crucify him." Pilate asked for a bowl of water and washed his hand saying, "I have no part in the blood of this man." His blood be upon us and upon our children", chorused the children of Israel. That was how the Israelites issued a generational curse upon themselves.

The Jews are still passing through that problem till date. Jerusalem was destroyed in a horrific manner. Blood flowed in the streets quenching the fire that was burning. The blood of Jesus Christ was actually upon them. Adolf Hitler killed six million Jews several years later. That was the most unprecedented massacre in the history of the world.

What the children of Israel had said (Matthew 27) has continued to work against them.

God can protect His people from curses but not from curses which are self-pronounced. If you issue curses against yourself, God will not protect you unless you are able to discover the sources of your problem, repent and cancel such curses.

This is one of the easiest ways which satan has continued to use to capture thousands of Christians.

Let us consider this fact from the Scriptures. Twelve spies were sent to spy out the land of Canaan. They carried out their assignments and came back with two types of report.

And Caleb stilled the people before Moses, and said, Let us go up at once, and possess it; for we are well able to overcome it. And they brought up an evil report of the land which they had searched unto the children of Israel, saying, The land, through which we have gone to search it, is a land that eateth up the inhabitants thereof; and all the people that we saw in it are men of a great stature. And there we saw the giants, the sons of Anak, which come of the giants: and we were in our own sight as grasshoppers, and so we were in their sight (Num 13:30,32,33).

Let us see what later happened.

And all the congregation lifted up their voice, and cried; and the people wept that night. And all the children of Israel murmured against Moses and against Aaron: and the whole congregation said unto them, Would God that we had died in the land of Egypt! or would God we had died in this wilderness! Num 14:1-.2).

What was God's reaction to all these?

And the LORD spake unto Moses and unto Aaron, saying, How long shall I bear with this evil congregation, which murmur against me? I have heard the murmurings of the children of Israel, which they murmur against me. Say unto them, As truly as I live, saith the LORD, as ye have spoken in mine ears, so will I do to you: Your carcases shall fall in this wilderness; and all that were numbered of you, according to your whole number, from twenty years old and upward, which have murmured against me, (Num 14:26- 29).

The ten spies and their followers determined their own destinies by the word of their mouths. *Your words can determine your destiny. It can even change Gods programme for your life.*

If you continue to curse yourself when God is blessing you, you will end up leading yourself into bondage. Many people have changed their destinies from what God intended them to be through self-imposed curses which came out of their mouths.

VERBAL MURDER

Do you know that people commit verbal murder, everyday? Let us examine examples of some of the statements which people generally make:

"I married a useless husband."
"These children are hopeless."
"I dont know why my children are very wicked."
"I always find examination very tough."
"I dont know why life is treating me badly."
"My blood pressure is rising again."
"My migraine is coming up again."
"This situation is driving me crazy."
"I am sick and tired of it all."

"It is running in the family line, maybe it is now my turn."

"I dont think I will ever get married."
"Maybe, I will never be promoted."

"Somebody read my palm and discovered that the line of long life does not get to the end of my hand. That means I am not going to live long. The same palm reader also said, The long line in your hand was crossed by three other lines. That means you are going to get married to three husbands. According to the word of that man, I should get ready to cope with three husbands and a short life."

"Something has always told me that my husband will leave me and marry other women."
"I just dont know why I cannot make ends meet. My father was like that, I am sure I am going to pass through the same problem."
"I am always broke, I dont know why."
"I dont know what is wrong, I always catch other peoples sicknesses."
"I suspect that I will soon get into trouble."
. "I have not always been lucky when it comes to male-female relationship."
"What is the use of continuing to live with all these problems?"
"Over my dead body. I cannot allow one child to kill me."
"Friends always disappoint me."

EVIL WORDS BRING EVIL SPIRITS

If you use these words, you are personally releasing some evil spirits into your life. The kind of evil spirits which will operate in your life will be determined by the kind of evil words which you have spoken concerning yourself. A lot of wicked evil spirits are hovering in the air and walking around on the land waiting for people to speak evil words which they will bring to pass.

I had an experience when I was a student in the University of Lagos, Nigeria. We had a very humble professor who was quite different from other lecturers. One day, the professor came around when we were doing a particular assignment and watched what we were doing. A female student who did not appear to be well-trained began to make some caustic statements about him. I said to her: "Mind what you are saying. Dont you know that he is our professor?" She turned deaf ears to what I was saying, faced the professor and said, "Mr. Man, get away from here. Your presence in this place has not allowed me to concentrate on my assignment."

The professor said, "Young lady, havent you learnt how to behave from home?" The lady became fierce and uncontrollable. "Foolish man", she said. Then the professor said "That is exactly what I was waiting for you to say. I was actually waiting for you to call me a foolish man so that I can prove to you that I am no fool." Immediately, the professor sent for the lecturer incharge of that course and said, "Tell this girl that she has failed the course." That was how the girl failed the course without sitting for the examination. What she said was used against her.

Evil spirits will provoke you to say evil things. As

soon you have made those evil statements they will go ahead to use your words against you. One of the reasons the spirits of death have continued to destroy peoples lives can be traced to the fact that such spirits were invited by the people.

Most of what people are told to say when they want to join secret cults is a perfect example of how people bring self-imposed curses upon themselves. They tell them; "Will you drink this blood and say, as I am standing on the ground now, the ground should begin to fight me if I reveal the secrets of this cult?" The person to be initiated drinks the blood and pronounces those words against himself. If the person runs away from the evil society, he would be in trouble because he has imposed those curses upon himself.

SOLUTION

If your father was a member of the Lodge, I will not be surprised if you are living under a serious curse now. Members of secret societies generally impose curses upon themselves and their children.

How can you release yourself from self-imposed curses?

Repentance - You must repent and acknowledge the fact that you have been saying wrong things against yourself.

Renouncement - Renounce what you have said. You must reject and withdraw what you said against yourself.

Revoke - You must revoke every evil statement which you uttered against yourself.

Replacement - You must replace every negative word pronounced against you. Replace evil words with good confessions. Replace satanic words with the promises of God.

What you have read so far is one of the greatest secrets which can turn your life around. It is worthy of prayer, meditation, repentance and action. No amount of speaking in tongues, fasting, prayer and positive confession can destroy self-imposed curses. The reason why some people are looking older than their ages is because they impose curses upon themselves.

Some husbands do not stay at home because their wives impose curses upon them. The reason some peoples businesses are collapsing can be traced to the kind of negative statements they made against themselves.

You must release yourself from the problem of self-destruction. You must take definite steps to set yourself free from the effect of every negative word which you pronounced upon yourself.

Have you ever taken an oath? Were you ever initiated into secret cults? You need personal deliverance. If you have spoken evil words against yourself, you must repent and ask God to forgive you.

PRAYER POINTS

1.   Make this personal confession: Lord Jesus, I come

before You today. I repent from every evil statement that I have pronounced on myself. I release myself from every evil oath that I have taken and from every evil vow that I have made. I stand on the Word of God that Jesus has redeemed me from the curse of the law. I release myself from every self-imposed curse, in the name of Jesus.

2. Make this statement seven times: I release myself from every self-imposed curse, in the name of Jesus.

3. I gather together every evil word that I have spoken against myself and I cancel them, in the name of Jesus.

4. Holy Spirit, always remind me to speak when You speak and be silent when You are silent, in the name of Jesus.

5. I renounce everything I said against myself when Iwas one year old, in the name of Jesus. I renounce everything I said against myself when I was two years old, in the name of Jesus. (Continue to renounce all the evil words which you spoke until your present age.)

6. All the condemnations which my mouth has invited, I cancel them, in the name of Jesus.

7. I command every spirit making me to say ungodly things to depart from me, in the name of Jesus.

4

Power against verbal disease

The greatest problems anyone can have on earth are those brought about by the tongue.

The Bible makes it very clear that the human tongue is responsible for most of the problems which men and women have today. Let us take a look at an incident in II Kings 2. The story, centres around Elisha, that man of God, after he had received the double portion of the power of God.

> **And he went up from thence unto Bethel: and as he was going up by the way, there came forth little children out of the city, and mocked him, and said unto him, Go up, thou bald head; go up, thou bald head. And he turned back, and looked on them, and cursed them in the name of the LORD. And there came forth two she bears out of the wood, and tare forty and two children of them (II Kings 2:23 -24).**

This passage shows us the demonstration of the power of the spoken word. The young children spoke some contemptuous words and Elisha spoke some words against them.

Why were the children killed by wild animals after Elisha cursed them in the name of the Lord? It is clear that the children were punished for the wrong use of their tongues. If you are a very good reader of the Bible you would have discovered that God generally takes urgent action whenever the issue at stake is both weighty and serious. The young children spoke words of mockery towards Elisha. What they said was pregnant with meaning. Their words of mockery were not only directed against Elisha it was also directed against Elijah, who ascended unto heaven through the chariot of fire.

Unknown to those young people, they violated a lot of spiritual principles. They were speaking against the power of God. Every reader of the Bible knows that Elijah was taken up to heaven through the raw demonstration of the power of God. To speak against such a miraculous event is an affront against the Almighty. More so, the young children were mocking Elisha saying that he should go up or ascend into heaven just the way his master did.

Additionally, they spoke against a man who had just received the double portion of the anointing saying, "Go up bald head."

It is clear that anyone who speaks against the servant of God is actually speaking against God. The fact that these young boys were from Bethel must be noted. Bethel was formerly the house of God. However, king Jerome had taken it over and converted it to the stronghold of idolatry. He placed an idol there and told Israel, "Behold, Israel, your God that delivered you from the land of Egypt." People started going to the house of the idol to worship it. Therefore, those boys were polluted because they came from Bethel, a place of idolatry. What they spoke with their mouths lent credence to what was in their hearts.

I want you to take this prayer point right now.

O Lord, forgive me for misuse of words against You.

Words are vehicles of power. There would have been no war in history if the whole humanity were dumb.

WORDS IN THE SCRIPTURES

There are three kinds of words in the Bible.

1. Words that carry positive power.

2. Words carrying negative power.

3. Neutral words.

Words are so powerful that the Bible says that death and life are in the power of tongue. The Bible says,

Let the words of my mouth, and the meditation of my heart, be acceptable in thy sight, O LORD, my strength, and my redeemer (Ps 19:14).

This shows that there are acceptable words, while there are unacceptable words.

Let us also read Job 4:4,

Thy words have upholden him that was falling, and thou hast strengthened the feeble knees (Job 4:4).

This shows us that power to strengthen the weak as well as power to uphold those who are falling can be found in the spoken word. The Bible gives us further insight into the power of the spoken word in Job 8:2:

> How long wilt thou speak these things? and how long shall the words of thy mouth be like a strong wind?

Words can be like strong wind blowing things here and there. Further insight is given us concerning the power of spoken words:

> How long will ye vex my soul, and break me in pieces with words? (Job 19:2).

What we are told in this passage is that words are so powerful that they can break people's lives into pieces.

The Bible says,

> I will worship toward thy holy temple, and praise thy name for thy lovingkindness and for thy truth: for thou hast magnified thy word above all thy name (Ps 138:2).

Words are so important to God that He magnified His word above His name. Proverb 18:4 also gives us more insight into the importance of the spoken word:

> The words of a man's mouth are as deep waters, and the wellspring of wisdom as a flowing brook.

This passage portrays the words of a man's mouth as deep waters.

Jesus, our Lord and Saviour, who says what He means, gave us one of the most challenging commentaries concerning the power of the human tongue in Matthew

12:37:

> **For by thy words thou shalt be justified, and by thy words thou shalt be condemned.**

If you are a very sound Bible reader, you would have discovered that if you are talking about blunt and straightforward speech you should read the word of Jesus. There is no iota of deception in His words. He also has this to say:

> **Heaven and earth shall pass away, but my words shall not pass away (Matt 24:35).**

The words of Jesus brought out the fact that certain words have eternal value. In other words, they cannot pass away.

TYPES OF WORDS IN THE SCRIPTURES

The Bible has a lot to say about words. The following types of words are listed in the scriptures.

1. Right words (Job 6:25).
2. Vain words (Exod. 5:9; 2 Kings 18:20, Job 16:3; Isa. 36:5; Eph. 5:6).
3. Words without knowledge (Job 35:16; 38:2).
4. False words (Zech. 8:17).
5. Pure words (Psalm 12:6).
6. Angry words (Neh. 5.6).
7. Roaring words (Psalm 22.1).
8. Words of iniquity (Psalm 36.3).

9. Devouring words (Psalm 52:4).

10. Soft words (Job 41:3).

11. Smooth words (Psalm 55:21).

12. Bitter words (Psalm 64:3).

13. Words of hatred (Psalm 109:3).

14. Flattering words (1 Thess. 2:5).

15. Sweet words (Prov. 23:8).

16. Words of knowledge (Prov. 19:27; 23:12; 1 Cor. 12:8).

17. Words of wisdom (1 Cor. 12:8).

18. Wicked words (Psalm 109:2).

19. Pleasant words (Prov. 16:26; 16:24).

20. Wounding words (Prov. 18:8).

21. Cursing words (Psalm 59:12).

22. Pursuing words (Proverbs 19:7).

23. Words of faith (1 Tim. 4:6).

24. Enticing words (1 Cor. 2:4; Col. 2:4).

25. Wrested words (Psalm 56:5).

26. Light-giving words (Psalm 119:130).

27. Words of understanding (Prov. 1:2).

28. Words of the wise (Prov. 22:1).

29. Multitude of words (Job 11:2; Prov. 10:19).

30. Grievous words (Prov. 15:1).

31. Words of truth (Prov. 22:21; Eccl. 12:10; Acts 26:25).

32. Hasty words (Prov. 29:20).

33. Words of vanity (2 Pet. 2:18).

34. Good words (1 Kings 12:7; 2 Chr. 10:7; Zech. 1:3; Rom. 16:18).
35. Sound words (2 Tim. 1:13).
36. Words taught by man's wisdom (Prov. 18:4).
37. Hard words (Psalm 94:4).
38. Unspeakable words (2 Cor. 12:4).
39. Wholesome words (1 Tim. 6:3).
40. The Words of God's power (Heb. 6:5).
41. Lying words (Isa. 32:7).
42. Gracious words (Luke 4:22).
43. Words of comfort (Isa. 50:4).
44. Strong words (Job 8:2).
45. Words without knowledge (Job 38:2).
46. Words of life (Phil. 2:6).
47. Words of truth (2 Tim. 2:15).

WHAT WORDS CAN DO

The types of words spoken by human beings are so diverse. The influence of words is so far-reaching and powerful that it takes God to protect us from the scourge of words. All these types of words are in the Bible. It is important, therefore, to know what to do if you happen to come under verbal attack.

The havoc brought into people's lives by negative words cannot be qualified. There is no living soul who has not been verbally harassed at one time or the other.

Examples of verbal attacks abound in the scriptures.

Haman harassed Mordecai through the use of words. Mordecai was arrested and he was supposed to face execution. Words were also spoken to reverse the situation. At the end, Haman was executed. That shows that words can kill and words can make alive.

A careless word may lead to a serious fight. Cruel words can lead people to commit suicide. Negative words may completely wreck a life. Wicked words can kill while gracious words can lead people to wonderful heights.

The words, which we speak, have great potentials for good as well as for evil for ourselves and for the people who we speak about. Therefore, the words, which we speak from day to day, hold great value both for ourselves and for the people who hear us.

It is unfortunate that we do not generally give sufficient attention to the power of our words, losing sight of the fact that our words have the ability to bless and to curse. Words can turn situations to our advantage. Our words can clarify situations and can also confuse situations. Your words can bring light into a place. They can also bring darkness into a situation. God stands by His own words. He also stands by our own words.

Another great truth which I want you to consider with all your heart is the fact that satan and his demons also pick up our words and use them to war against us. As I said in the previous chapter, the devil has no creative power, he relies on the evil creative words which are spoken consciously or carelessly by men and women. Therefore, the effects of spoken words can be devastating.

You must be careful about what you listen to, the kind of music which you listen to as a Christian. Some music can be used as a vehicle for blessing, cursing, or polluting the lives of men and women. A lot of people have been enslaved through music. Best selling records have been used by the devil to lead people into bondage.

There is a particular best selling song, which created one of the greatest impacts in the music industry. It was entitled "My good Lord." The song goes like this:

> My good Lord Hallelujah
> My good Lord Hallelujah
> I really want to see you Hallelujah
> I really want to love you Hallelujah
> My good Lord Hallelujah

That was what the musician was saying on the surface. However, he took a digression along the line saying:

> My good Lord (mentioning the name of his idol)

If you do not listen properly you will think that the man is saying Hallelujah not knowing that the song is dedicated to a cult. There are many songs like that particular one today. Such songs have been cleverly used by the devil to lead people into bondage.

AFRICAN PRAISE NAMES

There is a common practice in many African

communities. Families are given what is called praise names or praise-poems. If you are a member of a particular community or family, you are given some special praise-poems. This praise-poem generally eulogises the achievement of your ancestors, the exploits achieved by your family as well as the distinctiveness of your tribe.

Some African tribes are often proud of their praise names. The foundation poems are so popular that most Africans are proud of them. Words are composed and are rendered to praise men and women to bring out their nobility, honour and dignity as members of a particular tribe or family.

Many of us often enjoy such praise names as it brings out ego and pride. You must not look at those words as ordinary words. Those words are combinations of incantations, the history of your ancestors and the list of what they have achieved. Such praise names are rendered to make you feel that you are a member of a great race. That is part of the vanity of life.

A sister went through deliverance for a long time without experiencing any positive changes in her life. They prayed for her over and over again without achieving any tangible result. The man of God who was handling the case sought the face of God for an answer to the reason behind the difficult encounter by the sister in obtaining her deliverance. The Lord told him that, that sister cannot experience deliverance until some secrets, which were embedded in her praise-name, were exposed and dealt with by the Lord.

The man of God asked the sister. "Do you know anything about your personal praise name?" The sister said, "Yes. I' am thoroughly familiar with it." The man of God told her to recite her praise-poem and she did. Her fluency baffled the man of God. The sister went ahead to explain that she succeeded in memorizing the praise poem because it was customary for members of her family to recite it to her each time she wakes up in the morning.

The man of God asked her to recite the praise-poem once again. Then he noted a particular line, which goes thus: "The tree of your family never grows old." The man of God asked the sister. "Do you generally witness sudden deaths in your family?" She said, "We were 16 but now only four of us are alive." The Pastor then said: "Do you mean that you have continued to allow them to read that praise-poem to you even when almost all of you have died prematurely?"

At that point, the sister realised that one of the entry points of bondage into her life can be traced to her family's praise-name.

What kind of words do you speak about your life? What kind of things do you say about the lives of other people? When last did you say something ungodly about somebody? When last did you speak unkind words about other people? When last did you run somebody down through your tongue? When last did you lash out at somebody out of anger?

When last did you say something which you later regretted? When last did you join others to spread a rumour? When last did you backbite? When last did you swear using God's name? When last did you use the name of the Lord in vain? When last did you rain abuses and curses on a fellow human being? When last did you call somebody a derogatory name? You must answer these questions.

When last did you call somebody an idiot? Have you forgotten what the Bible says? That if you call someone an idiot you are in danger of judgement? Do you still abuse people by using caustic words?

I often get surprised when I come across people who throw caution to the winds and abuse everyone. I had a shocking experience several years ago when a mother cursed her own little child just because he made a little mistake. I was transfixed on the same spot when the mother cursed his son saying, "You will never have rest just the way a door has no rest." As if that was not enough, the mother cursed the boy the second time. She said, "Your life will be turned to a desert just as hair cannot grow on the palm." I had to caution her when it became clear that she did not know the implication of what she was saying. She laughed and said, "It is not a serious thing. I didn't really mean it." Have you ever abused someone in that manner?

When last did you enter into a shouting match with someone? When last did you pour acidic words on your husband or wife? When last did you grieve the Holy Spirit by speaking when He told you not to?

I shared this with you in the first chapter. Let me repeat it as a matter of emphasis. A man who was considered to be the wisest person in an empire was asked an important question. "What do you consider as the most powerful weapon, which can be used to control things in the world?" The wise man said, "There are only three things in the entire universe. Number one is the tongue. Number two is the tongue, while number three is also the tongue." Those who asked the question wondered if the man knew what he was saying. They later discovered that although the tongue is one of the smallest parts of the body, it is one of the most powerful members. Incidentally, it is the only part of the body that becomes sharper with constant use. Other parts of the body grow older while the tongue becomes sharper.

The tongue causes us more problems than any other part of the body. It can be tragically destructive. Unless the present day Christian receives the divine coal of fire on his tongue it will continue to hurt rather than heal.

Our words can destroy our relationships with our neighbours. Our own words can also turn our personal life upside down. The tongue can be likened to keeping a time bomb underneath one's bed. The result will be devastating when it explodes.

A careful study of the word of God reveals that the whole of creation was brought into being through the instrumentality of words. Nothing was created without the spoken word. The Rhema of God's word was the instrument which God used to bring the universe into existence. God said, "Let there be" and the world was brought into existence. Have you ever realised the fact that God transferred the same creative word to man by giving him the power of speech?

The creative ability which resides in our world should make us to exercise care and caution about what we speak about God, ourselves and fellow human beings.

The secrets of speaking the right words and achieving good results have been revealed to us by the Lord Jesus. He said,

> Either make the tree good, and his fruit good; or else make the tree corrupt, and his fruit corrupt: for the tree is known by his fruit. O generation of vipers, how can ye, being evil, speak good things? for out of the abundance of the heart the mouth speaketh. A good man out of the good treasure of the heart bringeth forth good things: and an evil man out of the evil treasure bringeth forth evil things (Matt 12:33-35).

Jesus relates our words to a tree and its fruits. What then is the importance of Jesus' statement? The heart is the tree while the fruit is the mouth. The tree is known by its fruit. Therefore, what comes out of your mouth is an indication of what is in your heart. Nobody ever makes accidental statements. Your mouth cannot declare what is not present in your heart. Therefore, if you want to know the state of your heart you must judge it by examining the kind of words that come out of your mouth.

VERBAL DISEASES

The Bible teaches that there are many verbal diseases. These verbal problems or diseases are so numerous that I may not be able to exhaust them in this chapter. Let us go through the most important verbal diseases.

Undisciplined tongue. This is perhaps one of the greatest problem of man. If you allow your tongue to run loose, you will run into lots of problems sooner or later.

Impatient tongue.

Unsympathetic tongue.

Fearful tongue.

Aimless tongue.

Unpredictable tongue.

Proud tongue.

Argumentative tongue.

It has been said that the marriage is one in which the wife is both deaf and dumb and the husband is blind. This will prevent the women from talking rubbish and prevent the man from seeing rubbish.

Repetitive tongue.

Unaffectionate tongue.

Inconsistent tongue.

Revengeful tongue.

Tactless tongue.

Disorganised tongue.

Stubborn tongue.

Suspicious tongue.

Critical tongue.

Reckless tongue.

Domineering tongue.

Talkative tongue.

Loud tongue.

Rash tongue.

I have decided to run through the list of the kinds of verbal diseases that have led men and women into hell fire. These verbal diseases have landed many into terrible problems, stolen the blessings of millions of people and sentenced many lives to permanent residence at the valley.

What you have read so far must have made you to know that you can consciously or unconsciously cage yourself through the words which you speak. I am sure you have discovered that you can consciously or unconsciously cage other people through the words you speak.

I want you to open your mouth like thunder as you take this prayer point:

I cancel every negative word that has proceeded from my mouth, in the name of Jesus.

I have an additional prayer point for you. Close your eyes and take it with more aggression:

Let the divine coal of fire fall upon my tongue now, in the name of Jesus.

OTHER VERBAL DISEASES

Now we shall take a detailed study of some of the verbal diseases.

Gossips. Gossips are destructive. Everyone who gossips is making himself or herself satan's broadcasting company. One of our rules of conduct in the ministry is this: If someone comes to tell you, "Are you aware of what Brother A. said about you?" Respond with this statement: "Can you repeat what you have just said in the presence of Brother A." If he says, "No, I don't want anybody to hear about it; I'm not ready to repeat this statement before Brother A," tell the person to go for deliverance straightaway.

What then is gossip? Gossip is anything you cannot say before a person, which you say behind that person. The person who gossips is not the only one who is guilty. He who listens to gossip is also guilty. Both of them are under the banner of judgement. One thing I have always said, time and again, is this those who bring gossips to you will also go to other people to gossip about you.

Christian gossips. It appears that Christians have perfected the art of gossiping in these last days. People now gossip intelligently. They do not want to accept the fact that they are gossiping. When such people want to spread gossips they call Christians together saying that they are holding a prayer meeting.

The gossip stands up to say, "Let us pray for Sister Jane. She has a serious problem. She lost ₦10,000 to fraudsters because she was careless. Let us pray that God will forgive her for her prayerlessness. Brethren, tell me, how can a fraudster dupe a child of God? In any case. God will forgive her. We really have to pray that God will have mercy on her. Who knows, God would have allowed her to be duped because she is fond of gossiping."

"Brethren, do you know that sister Jane has been a member of this church for five years without knowing how to pray to know the will of God? Sister Jane is already 36. She is supposed to be married by now but she is still single because she has always insisted on getting married to Brother Dave who is studying Architecture in America. Anyway, don't let me tell you a long story. Let's just pray for her."

"This reminds me, don't forget to pray that God will help her to be submissive to the leadership of the church. Sister Jane is so stubborn that she cannot be controlled by anyone. I don't know why she is that stubborn. Yet we all know what brought her to this church. Was she not the one who almost had mental problem and had to be rushed to the prayer warriors? Anyway don't let me talk too much. The whole church has already known that she is too close to Pastor Chukwu."

"We are going to really pray for sister Jane. We are not going to allow anybody to destroy this church. Although people have been saying that she is a marine agent, let us bind every spirit that is working contrary to her life. We are going to claim her for the Lord."

"Let us not forget to pray for the senior pastors, that God will give them wisdom to help Sister Jane. I m sure you know that the fact that someone is a senior pastor does not mean that the person is hearing from God. You must cry unto God aggressively today. The success of this church is in our hands. Let us lift Sister Jane up unto the Lord. Let us tell the devil 'enough is enough.'"

"Let us destroy all the strongholds in the life of Sister Janes family. We have heard that there is a stubborn yoke in the life of every member of her family. They always end up destroying any church they attend".

"Let us pray that God will expose Sister Jane if that is her mission in our church. We must also pray that God will remove worldliness from her life. Somebody once told me that she spent ₦5,000 on a pair of shoes. If any of you is in doubt, just watch her next Sunday. Only God knows why she is that proud".

"Why is she even proud? Is she not the same person who buys second hand blouses? We must pray for her. As you are praying for her dont forget to mention the name of Sister Agnes. She happened to be one of the most serious sisters in this church until she became sister Janes friend. Do you know that Sister Agnes is fond of gossiping about Pastors? Although some of the things she said are true. For example, she is the one who made us to start praying for Pastor Nsikak. Im sure you know that Sister Agnes was the one who made us to know that Pastor Nsikak's wife is prayerless. We must spend real time to pray for all these people".

"However, since our time is gone, let us take just one prayer point. I bind all satanic agents sent to the church of God, in the name of Jesus. Pray with thunder in your voice".

Do you think this picture is painted beyond the realms of reality? You cannot know how far some so-called Christians have gone in spreading gossips about fellow believers. Gossips have been ingrained to the lives of many people that it has become their second nature. The evil inherent in gossip can only be revealed when two gossip partners quarrel with each other. Then all the words, which they spoke as partners in gossip, will be blown into the open.

Most people who gossip find the evil habit interesting. They only detest gossip when they are victims. The best attitude toward gossip is to ignore it. If you know what you stand upon as a child of God, gossip will not bother you. This is my own attitude to gossips. I rejoice when people gossip about me. To be sure, people may not gossip about me if Im doing nothing for the Lord. But the fact that I am busy for the Lord has made me an object of gossip. You must expect people to gossip about you as long as you are alive.

My father went to be with the Lord in 1994. Nobody can gossip about him again. Therefore those of us who are alive will continue to be objects of gossip, especially when we are busy for the Lord. I feel sorry for those who have constituted themselves into satanic "F. M. stations".

Gossip is a very dangerous activity. When you gossip about somebody and the statement made by you turns out to be untrue, you bring yourself under divine judgement. It is much more dangerous if the person whom you are gossiping about is a man of God. His anointing and his angels may deal with you severely.

Rumours. Those who gossip often act in favour of the people whom they are gossiping about without knowing what they are doing. For example, God has used the gossips and the rumours spread against the Mountain of Fire and Miracles Ministries to give us an increase in the numerical strength of our membership. Some pastors in other churches have brought the awareness of what God is doing in our church to their members when such members know nothing about the existence of any church called Mountain of Fire and Miracles Ministries. They mount their pulpits and criticise Mountain of Fire and Miracles Ministries. They say so much about us that they end up arousing the curiosity of their members.

Some members who are intelligent call themselves together saying, "Is there a place like that in town? Let's check it out. After all, they have doors through which we can get out if what our pastor is saying is actually true".

A pastor came to us the other day to apologise

profusely for having said negative things about us. He actually came to look for somebody in the church. He decided to wait till the end of the service to meet his friend. However, the Holy Spirit convicted him. He sat down and cried for about 20 minutes, telling the Lord that he was sorry to have said negative things about us. He had preached to members of his congregation against coming to attend our church without ever visiting us before. He told them that we did not preach holiness, that we were always drinking oil, that we were not Christians.

Incidentally, we were preaching on brokenness the very day he came. He came to us and said that he had never had a such message throughout his 15 years of being in the ministry. Thank God he had an opportunity to make amends. Who knows what would have happened to him if he had died without a first hand experience in our service.

You must learn a lesson from the experience of this pastor. You must repent of all the negative things, which you once said about men of God and other Christian ministries.

Slander. What is a slander? Simply put, it is an intentional and open sharing of damaging information concerning a person or group of persons. The Bible says,

> Thou shalt not go up and down as a talebearer among
> thy people: neither shalt thou stand against the blood
> of thy neighbour: I am the LORD (Lev 19:16).

Many peoples lives have been destroyed through slander. You must not allow or partake in slander. Refuse to listen to those who go about slandering other people.

Lying. Lying is one of the most serious verbal diseases that destroyed the lives of people. The Bible says,

> These six things doth the LORD hate: yea, seven are
> an abomination unto him: A proud look, a lying
> tongue, and hands that shed innocent blood, An heart
> that deviseth wicked imaginations, feet that be swift
> in running to mischief, A false witness that speaketh
> lies, and he that soweth discord among brethren
> (Prov 6:16 19).

Do you notice that of these seven things, which constitute an abomination to the Lord, three are related to the tongue?

Proverbs 12:22 further clarifies the issue.

> Lying lips are abomination to the LORD: but they that
> deal truly are his delight.

The word abomination is the strongest word which

can be used to describe something hated by God. Lying is highly inconsistent with Christian character. God expects us to speak the truth at all times. Someone has said that sin has several tools but a lie is the handle that picks up the tool. When you lie against the truth you are strengthening satan's stronghold in your life.

The Bible states that satan is the father of all lies. Therefore, falsehood or lying is the devil's language. Satan is the chief promoter of lying. A lie is the opposite of the truth. All those who are telling lies are supporters and promoters of satan's system. Some people are so addicted that they can be said to possess the anointing of lying. A lie may run a race for 50 years, truth will catch up with it in one second.

Speaking negative words. The worst disease, which you can bring upon yourself, is speaking negative words about life. Let us take a look at a particular example in the Scriptures.

Then answered all the people, and said, His blood be on us, and on our children (Matt 27:25).

They made a statement which has continued

to affect them up till today. Negative speaking is a popular disease. It is a respectable sin. Many people hardly consider the fact that it is a terrible disease.

We were praying for a sister in London because she wanted to receive the baptism of the Holy Spirit. She kept on making negative confessions. She did not receive the baptism of the Holy Spirit until she changed her confessions.

I used to have a Zimbabwean classmate when I was in England. He had a ready answer for me each time I said "How are you?" His reply was, "The struggle continues."

Twelve spies went to spy out the Promised Land. Ten of them made negative confessions while Caleb and Joshua said, "We are well able." Those who were involved with negative speaking did not enter the Promise Land. That is how many people have cancelled their blessings through the wrong use of their mouth.

Boasting and flattery. Those who boast generally centre conversations around themselves. They praise and lift themselves up beyond the level they are. Many people, including men of God, have allowed themselves to be destroyed by flattery.

I had a funny experience when I was invited to preach in a particular fellowship. Somebody called me and said, "Dr. Olukoya, you have really made it." I protested: "O what do you mean by that statement? How many people are in Lagos? " The man answered, "Between three and five million people." I threw another question at him. "How many people were in that meeting? " The man answered, "About 150." "What then have I made?" I asked him.

In my own opinion you can only say that you have made it as a Nigerian preacher if you have about 50 million people in your church.

Boasting is generally the promotion of vanity. Do you have anything to boast of? What have you achieved that another person has not achieved? What do you possess that others have not possessed before? There is nothing wrong if somebody tells you, "We thank God for what God is doing through you." That is an ordinary complement. But if someone says, "Let's give a round of applause to one of the greatest men of God who has ever lived." That one is flattery.

Excessive talking. Excessive talking is a door-way that leads to multitude of sins. The Bible says

In the multitude of words there wanteth not sin: but he that refraineth his lips is wise (Prov 10:19).

Ecclesiastics 5:3 also says:

For a dream cometh through the multitude of business; and a fool's voice is known by multitude of words.

According to the standard of the Bible a talkative is a fool.

There is an inseparable link between a reckless tongue and a reckless heart. Those who speak without thinking can be likened to soldiers who shoot without aiming at any targets.

I had a lecturer when I was doing my Ph.D. Who used to tell us, "Don't use a gallon of words to express a spoonful of thoughts".

The Bible says,

> Seest thou a man that is hasty in his words? there is more hope of a fool than of him (Prov 29:20).

The more words you speak, the less sensible you become.

Being hasty in speech. Be slow to speak, do not say what comes to your mind immediately you feel like saying it. Those who generally speak hastily always make mistakes. That was Moses' sin. He spoke hastily. God dealt with him because he was hasty.

Using God's name in vain. Exodus 20:7 says,

> Thou shalt not take the name of the LORD thy God in vain; for the LORD will not hold him guiltless that taketh his name in vain (Exod 20:7).

To use God's name as if it has no worth or value before you is to sin against God. If you call the name of God as if you are calling the name of someone who is inferior to you, you are degrading God. To say, "O God", when there is really nothing to say about God, amounts to taking the name of the Lord in vain.

STEPS TO HEALING

What then is the solution to the problem of verbal

diseases? How can you deal with your tongue? What must you do to escape the danger of hell?

Recognise the fact that a sick tongue shows that there is a problem in your heart. Do you know that the heart is the barometer for measuring the tongue? You can only have a wholesome tongue when your heart is wholesome. If you have a verbal disease in your tongue you can be sure that your heart is also full of diseases. It must be cleansed by the blood of Jesus and renewed by the word of God. It must be sanctified.

Confess your sins and ask for cleansing and forgiveness.

Resist evil and yield to God. Withdraw your tongue from satans grip.

Determine, by the help of the Holy Spirit, to use your tongue aright. Make up your mind that you will not say anything without allowing the Holy Spirit to sanction or condemn your word.

Let your mouth be filled with praises to God. If you commit your lips to the praise of God at all times you will find it difficult to utilise the same mouth to say bad things.

Be crucified. Brokenness will lead you into wonderful changes. Once your life is broken, your tongue will begin to speak words that glorify God.

What God expects from you is a change of life. God will not judge you on the bases of what you know. Rather, He will judge you on the basis of what you do with what you know. The judgement of God will be greater for anyone who knows the truth and fails to do it.

Are you ready to surrender your tongue to the Lord? Are you willing to banish all forms of lying, boasting and flattery from your tongue? Will you continue to spread gossips and rumours after going through this book?

Are you ready to apologise to those whom you have slandered? Will you allow the Lord to set a watch over your lips? Will you allow your tongue to take you to hell fire?

God wants you to make this day a turning point in your life. You must repent of all the ways in which you have misused your tongue. This is your hour of decision. Now is the time to cry unto God. Pray as if the Lord is coming after this session of prayer.

PRAYER POINTS

1. I break the power of any evil word uttered against me, in the name of Jesus.

2. I release myself from self-imposed curses, whether it is conscious or unconscious, in the name of Jesus.

3. O Lord, do not allow my mouth to push me into hell fire.

4. Let every satanic anchor working against me be roasted, in the name of Jesus.

5

The strife of tongues

For a proper understanding of this message we shall begin with two powerful scriptures:

Thou shalt hide them in the secret of thy presence from the pride of man: thou shalt keep them secretly in a pavilion from the strife of tongues (Ps 31:20).

Set a watch, O LORD, before my mouth; keep the door of my lips (Ps 141:3).

These two passages have a lot to say about the human tongue. The first reference borders on the importance of seeking protection from the strife of tongues. The second centres on the importance of setting a watch over ones lips.

There is a very dangerous door, which has caused most destructions in our present world. The unfortunate thing about that door is that it has no lock. The world would have been a better place if many people did not possess that door. God in His wisdom has designed the human head with economy. He gave us two openings each in areas that portend no danger: two eyes, two ears, two nostrils. But there was a change when God came to a unique area, the mouth. God gave us one mouth. Who knows what would have happened if we were created with two mouths and two tongues. The universe would have been besieged by verbal wars.

We have a lot of messages to learn from the way God created openings in the head. The divine economy that is displayed in the way that the tongue is created should teach us some lessons. You must be thrifty in the use of your tongue. You must not say anything that is unnecessary. God wants you to hear twice and speak once. He wants you to hear properly and see things well before you ever speak about them. Some people talk as if they have two mouths. If a tax were to be placed on the number of words which we speak, many of us would have become bankrupt. Who knows, many people would have been bankrupt but they do not know.

POWER BEHIND WORDS

Whatever God tells us is for our utmost good. God would not tell us anything that is absolutely not necessary. Unknown to us, most of the commandments given to us by God are for our physical and material well-being. It is important, therefore, that we should listen to Him at all times.

The Bible says,

Come, ye children, hearken unto me: I will teach you the fear of the LORD. What man is he that desireth life, and loveth many days, that he may see good? Keep thy tongue from evil, and thy lips from speaking guile. (Ps 34:11 13).

Here, the Bible tells us that the tongue plays a very crucial role in our lives. The Bible also tells us that:

Whoso keepeth his mouth and his tongue keepeth his soul from troubles (Prov 21:23).

You must keep yourself from trouble by exercising caution over what you say.

There is a powerful secret behind the nature of words, which man has failed to realise over the ages. Words are not just spoken. Most of what we say are backed up by some powers. The power could be evil and it could be good. What this simply means is that the words which we speak have spirit beings behind them. Words do not exist in isolation; they carry power.

How did the serpent lead Adam and Eve into bondage? He did so by speaking words to them. He projected his lying nature through his words. What the serpent spoke to our fathers in the Bible has continued to cause trouble for all of us.

Words go beyond the arrangement of letters. They can be likened to a container which can be filled with poisonous substances or things that can grant us good health. The container can be filled with things like: anger, malice, envy, cursing or destruction.

Most of your past and present troubles were brought into reality through words, which were carelessly spoken by you. Just as you took some time to ¬peak those negative words, you must also spend quality time reversing them.

You cannot go through this book without taking a second look at the kind of words which you have been speaking. Words are so powerful that once they are spoken they continue to produce all kinds of fruits. I wish it where possible for you to record every word spoken by you and listen to them everyday. What is happening to you today is a product of what you said yesterday.

Your words will determine your destiny. You must weigh your everyday conversation and learn how to keep quiet sometimes instead of talking all the time.

Words do not die but live forever. A war of words is presently going on in our planet.

Words can summon good or bad spirits. Those who speak evil words can also be affected by what they say. If you curse others you will also reap the fruits of the wicked words which you speak. Those who speak angry words will always invite violent and wicked spirits into their own lives. If you come across men who have spirit wives you will discover that most of them are people who easily get angry and politicians who speak words of deceit.

Politicians speak deceptive words to the populace. Leaders of nations, all over the world, are speaking words of disunity, war and chaos. Leading academics are speaking words of blasphemy against the Almighty. Demonic musicians are speaking words that destroy the lives of men and women.

I remember a musician who sang a song in praise of one wealthy man. He stated in his song that the wealthy man would not die. However, the wealthy man died only a few months later.

False prophets are speaking words of destruction and doom. Ministers of dry cathedrals are speaking dry, lifeless words. They minister death to dying people and speak stale words to stale ears. Satan and his agents are speaking words of lying and destruction to unstable souls. That is why the Bible says,

Either make the tree good, and his fruit good; (Matt 12:33).

The Bible also tells us that men shall give account of every idle word that they speak on the Day of Judgment. It states specifically,

By thy words thou shall be justified and by thy words thou shall be condemned.

Every ungodly word, which you speak, is recorded. Since a man speaks out of the abundance of his heart, a carnal man will speak carnal words while a spiritual man will speak spiritual words.

Your words reveal the type of person you are, it is the best commentary on your personality and character. Show me a man who is dignified, God fearing and disciplined and I will show you a man who will speak sober words. Show me a man who is morally bankrupt, loose and ungodly and I will show you a man who will speak words that are unreasonable, dirty and ungodly.

You can try to cover up what is in your heart but words

will soon reveal the stuff you are made of.

A man cannot be separated from his words. Some people try to deny their words not knowing that words go beyond ·the physical realm. There is a spiritual attachment between you and your words. You cannot run away from your words. The tongue is so powerful that God had to make a very important statement about it.

> **Thou shalt hide them in the secret of thy presence from the pride of man: thou shalt keep them secretly in a pavilion from the strife of tongues (Ps 31:20).**

No doubt God must have recognised the enormity of the dangers inherent in the strife of tongues that He has to provide a spiritual shelter for His people. For God to hide or to protect anyone from something, that particular thing must be very powerful.

One of the most serious wars which can ever take place on earth, is the war of words. A lot of people are addicted to African video films because they centre around the war of words.

Wars are preceded by war of words. If men are going to destroy themselves with bombs and missiles, they are going to begin with the war of words. Two nations cannot fight each other if their leaders have not had a verbal war.

CAUSES OF STRIFE OF TONGUES IN AFRICA

What constitutes the strife of tongues in the African environment? What can we call the strife of tongues in our local setting?

Cursing - Curses are so rampant in the African environment that the majority terms it a plaything. The most important feature of a curse is that it goes to the root once it is invoked. Can you recall that immediately Jesus cursed the fig tree it dried from the roots? The roots of many lives have been dried up through curses. Many people have accumulated so many curses that their lives have completely withered. Some people have more than enough curses in their lives that the possibility of experiencing success and wholesomeness is completely ruled out.

The lives of many people were finished when they were very young. Neighbours and parents rained enough curses on them to render them useless for life. It is so saddening that so many people have received curses that will restrict them to the valley no matter what they do.

It is important to note that a lot of Africans have received enough curses from their immediate families that they do not need any external curses again.

It is also important to note that many people in Africa might have received curses before they attained the age of ten than a person from either America or Britain who is 80 years old.

When an African child does something wrong, the

parents would likely make statements like "It shall not be well with you." "Your head is cursed." "Just as the hinges of the door have no rest, your life will have no rest." "You will suffer like the soles of a shoe." "You shall carry the evil you are trying to do to me with your own head." "People of the world have destroyed your life." "The god of iron will kill you." Etc.

However, if the child of a white man misbehaves he simply says, "Don't be stupid." "Don't be naughty", and so on. This explains why most white people are prospering while Africans find it difficult to achieve success with ease.

The situation is even worse when Africans invoke curses on their children in the name of their gods. Africans make statements like: "Amadiora, (the god of thunder) will strike your head." "Sango, (the god of thunder) will strike you." "The ground on which you stand will stand against you." Etc.

A couple had a little domestic misunderstanding. The wife asked for money to make soup for the family and the husband handed her ₦20 (an equivalent of 20 cents in American currency). The woman threw the money back at him saying, "What kind of soup am I going to make with ₦20?" The man simply said, "That's all I have. You must manage that money." "Manager," she said. "It's okay. You are going to have problems that will make you to spend until you begin to borrow." That was a curse.

The man thought it was a joke. He did not know that

the wife had invoked a curse on him. That was the beginning of problems in his life. He began to have nightmares and all kinds of spiritual attacks. Some invisible people were whipping him daily. He felt real pain but he did not see anybody. That attack brought strange sicknesses to his body. He spent a lot of money until he became a debtor. He kept on borrowing until no one was ready to give him a loan. He became tired of himself and even thought of taking his life. However, a kind neighbour brought him to the church. That was how the yoke was broken. The man would have died in that process if not for divine intervention.

A lot of women traders are unable to make profit in business because of the curses placed upon them by their husbands.

Hot exchange of words - When evil words are spoken, they cause lots of havoc because they are backed up by evil powers. That is why it is not right to speak whenever you are angry. It is not proper to argue with people who have authority over you. It is also not proper to argue with anointed men of God. They might speak angry words which will do a lot of havoc in you or in your life.

Evil words can come from angry exchange of words. All those who are filled with the Holy Ghost should avoid hot verbal exchanges.

Incantations - Simply put, incantations are invitations given out by human beings to demonic spirits to punish a person. It centres on the invocation of demonic powers to destroy or harm another person.

Incantations have been handed over to succeeding generations in Africa. The African continent was so dark that men and women destroyed one another through the use of incantations. Those who chant incantations go beyond the realm of ordinary words. They appeal to the demonic realm through words that are carefully selected according to the dictates of evil powers.

Immediately incantations are released, evil spirits are activated. When evil people faced anyone as their opponent they begin by chanting incantations against the person.

Incantations are used as weapons of inviting evil spirit to participate in the lips of men. Those who chant incantations actually do so to take the battle beyond the physical realm.

Evil reports - Evil reports are also part of the strife of tongues. Somebody is offended and he decides to take that case to a very powerful fetish priest.

Cases are also taken to false prophets, occult societies and other demonic places as a means of punishing someone who offends them. When they get to those who are supposed to harm their opponents they make statements like: "This is what so and so did to me. If I don't get rid of this idiot he will continue to harass me." Many lives have been destroyed through such evil reports.

Thousands are roaming the streets as mad men and

women because their cases were taken to evil places and evil report was made concerning them. Thousands have had accidents, lost huge amount of money, husbands, children, jobs and other valuable property.

Careless use of abusive language - A lot of people use abusive language when they are playing with colleagues or family members. Abusive language is not as simple as it appears on the surface. A lot of evil spirits are attached to abusive words.

When you use words like, "You are stupid", "You are a goat", "Foolish man", "You are an idiot", "You are numskull", "You are a dog," "I cannot discuss with a toad like you," "You are an animal", "Your brain is like the brain of a cockroach", you are into the strife of tongues.

If you play with abuses, deriding parts of people's body by saying; "Look at his head or look at his legs", you are involved in the strife of tongues.

Reversal of words - It is common to some people to reverse words when they know that they mean exactly the opposite of what they are saying. The external reversal of words that mean evil internally is another wrong use of words. Those who say this kind of words actually know that what they wanted to say is bad but they say the exact opposite outwardly. Some parents say: "Who are those good children who are disturbing the peace of the home with their noises?"

What those parents actually mean is that bad children are disturbing the family. There is a contrast between what they meant and what they said. That is another example of strife of tongues. The devil works on what you mean not what you say.

Demonic charms - What do we mean by demonic charms? The Bible says:

> **And when they shall say unto you, Seek unto them that have familiar spirits, and unto wizards that peep, and that mutter: should not a people seek unto their God? for the living to the dead? (Isa 8:19).**

Charm is a highly sophisticated method used by demonic people to attack their victims. This method is mostly used by occult people.

I came across such a situation when I was in England several years ago. I used to notice a particular house each time I took a walk along a particular street. The house was always quiet. There was no sign of life there. One day, a classmate of mine told me, "Daniel, look at that house. Have you observed that the house is always quiet?" "Yes, I'm quite aware of that." I assured him. There was no single person in that house.

However, it shocked me when my friends said that a Nigerian was living in the topmost flat of the house. He said, "Let me tell you a story. The man who lives in that flat came from Nigeria to do his Ph.D. programme. I'm sure you know that he is supposed to spend three years. Now, he has been on that programme for eight years. That is why you have never seen him. He locks himself indoor most of the time. Enemies have dealt with him. He doesn't want to see anybody. His white supervisors and lecturers are tired of him. They always picked holes in whatever he wrote."

From that day I began to pray for him. I sought the face of the Lord and decided to help him. I went to his house one day, knocked at the door and struck a conversation with him. I shared the gospel with him and I also spent time to declare the power of the deliverance that resides in the name of Jesus. He thanked me and told me that he actually listened to me out of much regard. He made it very clear that he does not entertain any visitor. I thanked him and I left.

What I saw touched my heart. I decided to do everything to help him. His situation was so pathetic. His wife drew a lot of empathy and sympathy from me. Although she was in her early 30s, she looked like a 50 year old woman. No doubt the travails of her husband had taken a heavy toll on her. I took his case to God in prayer and I kept on bombarding heaven until God showed me the secret of his problem.

The Lord revealed to me that there was someone behind what the man was going through, that a wicked neighbour was chanting his name on a daily basis with the aim of destroying his life.

I decided that I was going to locate the demonic man who was responsible for the difficulties encountered by the Ph.D. student. Although what I wanted to do appeared risky, I didn't look at the risk involved. Rather, I was bent on bringing an end to the travails of the Nigerian student. The neighbour who was living downstairs welcomed me in spite of the fact that he did not know anything about me. I simply told him that I came to share the gospel with him. The man looked down on me and said that I was too small to be a Ph.D. student. He advised me to face my studies rather than preaching to people from house to house.

He spoke about a wide range of issues. Along the line, he veered into a subject of much interest to me when he said, "I don't take nonsense from anyone. If anyone falls into my trap, I deal with him mercilessly. For example, there is a man who is living in this building who calls himself a Ph.D. student. He went beyond his bounds. I have dealt with him. His case is closed. As long as I'm in England, he will never finish his Ph.D. programme. I've finished him."

I listened with rapt attention while he spoke. Everything he said confirmed what the Lord had spoken to me. I told the occult man that he should disregard all those powers and give his life to Jesus. I even went ahead to tell him that I could nullify all those things with prayer. His closing remark was "Don't trouble the powers of darkness." I thanked him for giving me an audience and left.

As soon as I left him, I began to think about what I was going to do concerning the situation. The Lord had made me to understand he spent one whole year doing a sort of demonic night vigil against the Ph.D. student. It became clear to me that night vigils must be carried out in the house of the Ph.D. student if what was programmed against him must be nullified.

If I decided to hold night vigils with the student and the occult man got to know about it he would view my action as conspiracy or betrayal of trust. I therefore decided to spend some time with the wife of the Ph.D. student since she was not under any siege.

I drilled her in the area of warfare until she became trained enough to handle her husband's problem. She started praying on her own, releasing her husband from powers that are taking hold of his life. As soon as the man began to calm down, he joined her in warfare prayers. They began to wake up 1.00 every night praying to break the yoke which occult powers had placed on the shoulders of the Ph.D. student. Their prayer every night was "Every charm and occult incantations coming from downstairs, be nullified, in the name of Jesus."

Within a few weeks, the student received a letter from his department asking him to come and defend his thesis. He was successful and awarded a Ph.D. degree. That was how God put an end to his problem. Meanwhile, the occult man became so offended that he did not want to see me again.

Occult members abound today. They appear as normal human beings during the day and spend the hours of the night chanting people's names for evil purposes.

Self-directed curses or swearing for the purposes of denying an allegation or claiming innocence -

Whenever an allegation is leveled against someone and the person denies it, it is customary for such people to be taken before local shrines to ascertain the truth of the matter.

There are certain powerful idols in Africa, which are meant for swearing. Whenever people are in dispute or whenever an allegation is denied, the person is taken before a shrine and made to invoke the power of the gods against himself or herself. Such a person would say, "If I am the one who stole the goat, may the idol of this village destroy me within seven days."

There are two dangers in that kind of swearing. If the person happens to be guilty in that matter, he will face the judgement of the demonic idol. He stands the risk of being destroyed or harmed by the idol. The devil is very wicked. You may make a statement saying, "If I have a hand in this matter let this idol reduce my life to a casualty and wreck. Let me not see good days on earth. Let my name become a bye-word in this community. Let my children die one after the other." Such a very powerful way of swearing is not as simple as it appears. The devil will ignore your first statement, "If I have any hand on this matter." He will hold you guilty for standing before an idol and invoking such terrible curses upon yourself.

That is exactly the reason the Bible says:

> But I say unto you, Swear not at all; neither by heaven; for it is God's throne: Nor by the earth; for it is his footstool: neither by Jerusalem; for it is the

city of the great King. Neither shalt thou swear by thy head, because thou canst not make one hair white or black. But let your communication be, Yea, yea; Nay, nay: for whatsoever is more than these cometh of evil (Matt 5:34-37).

We have a lot of lessons to learn from the passage.

1. *Do not swear by heaven.* A lot of people are fond of raising one finger to the sky and swearing. That habit is a clear violation of the word of God. It is not only a clear contradiction of the word of God it is also demonic. If care is not taken, hands which are raised up in that manner will never achieve anything good in life.

2. *It is wrong to swear by the earth.* Some people swear saying, "May the ground, on which I am standing fight against me if, . . ."

3. *It is wrong to swear by the name of your city or community.*

4. *It is wrong to swear by your head.* Those who say, "Let my head be anchored to evil if I am guilty in this matter." Such words are capable of destroying your destiny in life.

5. *You must avoid all forms of swearing.* Affirm your words by saying yea or nay. Thank God the international law permits anyone who wants to avoid swearing to affirm his or her words.

From the foregoing, it is crystal clear that you do yourself a lot of spiritual havoc whenever you utter evil statements against yourself in the name of swearing. The situation is more dangerous if you swear when you know that you are actually the offender. You must desist from all kinds of swearing today. Don't allow anybody to make you hold an iron in your hand or to bite it, saying that you are swearing by the god of iron. Don't allow anyone to make you do anything in the name of swearing. Let your yes be yes and your no be no.

Acceptance of demonic prophecy - If a prophet comes before you and gives you all kinds of evil prophecies, you must not accept such demonic words. How can a man who has ten wives, living an ungodly life, and has no single touch with God, tell you that you are going to have an accident, or that somebody close to you is going to die? Why should you accept such an evil prophecy?

What some of these prophets actually do is to direct curses at people's lives in the name of prophecy. They confuse you by telling you that what they uttered is in the mind of God.

Let us look at an example of how curses were concealed in the Scriptures. The curse was sent back to its sender. Let us read I Kings 18:17-18:

> **And it came to pass, when Ahab saw Elijah, that Ahab said unto him, Art thou he that troubleth Israel? And he answered, I have not troubled Israel; but thou, and thy father's house, in that ye have forsaken the commandments of the LORD, and thou hast followed Baalim.**

Jesus also countered what the devil said to him knowing that words are powerful. According to Matthew 4:4-5:

> And when the tempter came to him, he said, If thou be the Son of God, command that these stones be made bread. But he answered and said, It is written, Man shall not live by bread alone, but by every word that proceedeth out of the mouth of God.

Jesus countered the devil's word and gave him a knock out in the first round. Then the second round:

> Then the devil taketh him up into the holy city, and setteth him on a pinnacle of the temple, And saith unto him, If thou be the Son of God, cast thyself down: for it is written, He shall give his angels charge concerning thee: and in their hands they shall bear thee up, lest at any time thou dash thy foot against a stone (verses 5-6).

Here, the devil attempted to get Jesus into a wrong action by quoting the word of God in a wrong manner. The promise of the Scriptures centers on the protection of God's people. Such a protection was not meant for those who tempt the Lord. Jesus knew this and He did not fall into the temptation.

> Jesus said unto him, It is written again, Thou shalt not tempt the Lord thy God (verse 7).

The devil went to the third stage of the verbal war:

> Again, the devil taketh him up into an exceeding high mountain, and sheweth him all the kingdoms of the world, and the glory of them; And saith unto him, All these things will I give thee, if thou wilt fall down

and worship me (verses 8-9).

Jesus countered the devil's word:

> Then saith Jesus unto him, Get thee hence, Satan:
> for it is written, Thou shalt worship the Lord thy God,
> and him only shalt thou serve (verse 10).

HOW TO COUNTER-ATTACK STRIFE OF TONGUES

What do you do whenever there is a strife of tongues against you? You must take these three steps.

1. You must *reject*.

2. You must *reverse.*

3. You must *return*.

The use of acronyms is for easy memory. The first step you must take if you want to deal with strife of tongues is to reject such negative words. You must declare that evil words are not meant for you, that is how to reject such negative words. You must return all negative words to the sender. You must also reverse all negative words that are against you.

However, the most terrible and the worst of all situations of the strife of tongues is self-directed strife of tongues. It is not easy to deal with any strife of tongues which takes its origin from you. God cannot even help you if you are the one speaking evil against yourself. The only time when God will help you is when you stop saying negative things against yourself.

Those who speak negative words against themselves are guilty of self-destruction. You cannot blame any enemy for such an exercise in self-destruction. You are the one harassing yourself. You must therefore watch your words before your speak them.

Do you speak words of power? Do you speak words of weakness and condemnation? Do you speak words of love? Do you speak words of hatred? Do you center your words on bondage?

Do you speak words of victory and freedom? Do you speak words of life or death? Have you brought diseases and problems into your life through the words you spoke? Do you speak words of joy or sadness?

If you do not watch your words you will certainly limit the miracles of God in your life.

You must also ask yourself the following questions:

What kind of words am I speaking? Do I weigh my words? Am I a talkative? Am I chatting away my anointing?

If you have ever read church history, you would have discovered that all the powerful men of God were quiet people.

It is unfortunate that the enemies of our souls have learnt the secret of evil use of words. They issue curses, chant incantations and do all kinds of terrible things. What these evil powers invoke on men and women are so effective that God has promised that He would hide His people from the strife of tongues.

For example, God had to intervene when Balaam was hired by the enemies of the children of Israel to curse the children of Israel. If Balam's curse was not very serious and if it was not going to function, God would not have intervened. God intervened because He knew that a lot of evil and destruction were inherent in those words.

Let me give you a few tips before ending this chapter. You must be able to speak and neutralize any evil word spoken against you. You must not support the devil in speaking evil against your own life. Avoid words of doubt and condemnation. Speak words of deliverance. Do not speak words of bondage to your life. Avoid words of sickness and death. Speak words of healing to yourself.

Trade words of prosperity for words of poverty; words of commendation for words of condemnation; words of strength for words of weaknesses; words of success for words of failure; words of grace for idle words and words of life for words of death.

You must change your words from today. Instead of saying "Not too bad" when someone asks you, "How are you", you must learn to say, "It is well with me, in the name of the Lord." If your colleague asks you "How are you doing?" do not say, "I don't know what is happening to me, nothing is working." Rather you must say "God is good to me and God is doing great things in my life." Don't allow your mouth to utter any evil statement against you.

Instead of looking at your wife or husband and saying, "What's wrong with this bastard?" You must learn to say "How blessed am I to have married such a man or a woman like you."

I remember the case of a particular lady whose mother always abused her saying, "You are a bastard." True to the words of the mother the young girl got pregnant and did not know which of the three men who were having affairs with her was the father of the child.

You must rediscover the power of the spoken word today. You must walk in the same shoes with men of God who moved with God in the Scriptures. These men learnt the secret behind the spoken word. You must become wise today. Do not allow the enemy to trap you.

God is looking for an army of believers who will not only control their mouths but go ahead to employ the power of the spoken word in this end time warfare programme. Let me end this chapter with a Spanish proverb: "Flies do not get into a closed mouth."

PRAYER POINTS

1. Any curse issued against me to make people ask where is my God, return to the sender, in the name of Jesus.

2. I reject, reverse and recall every strife of tongues against my life, in the name of Jesus.

3. I release myself from every evil incantation past or present, in the name of Jesus.

4. Every misuse of my tongue against myself, I cancel it, in the name of Jesus.

5. Every power and activity of serpentine spirit against my life, be cancelled, in the name of Jesus.

6. Every evil report about me, I cancel you, in the name of Jesus.

6

Holiness and the tongue

I am sure you are no longer in the dark concerning the fact that it is possible to be trapped by the tongue.

The previous chapters have shown that a lot of people are under bondage, because they are trapped by their tongues. Many people have surrendered their mouth to the devil to be used as an instrument of destruction, disunity, discord, disaffection, rumour mongering, and sowing discord among the brethren. A lot of people who profess to know the Lord have allowed the devil to use them as evil messengers in the church, in the community and their personal families. Unless the issue of the tongue is fully dealt with, the devil will continue to keep many people under bondage.

The problem of the tongue can be traced to lack of personal holiness in the heart. If you are truly holy within and without, you will be able to keep your tongue under control. Your watchword at all times will be: what will Jesus say if He were in my shoes?

What is the key to wholesome living ? How can a Christian live a life of holiness before man and God ? The Bible says,

If any man among you seem to be religious, and bridleth not his tongue, but deceiveth his own heart, this man's religion is vain (James 1:26).

I have discovered, after several years of being in the Lord and observing the details of what happens within the body of Christ, that the greatest hindrance to living a holy life is inability to control the tongue. The greatest problems which many Christians have in this generation is the problem of unbridled tongue. Most Christians who profess the holiness experiences, belittle their profession and confession, as a result of their inability to exercise control over their tongues.

If you examine the Bible and church history you will discover that a lot of damage has been done in the church of God and in the world by men and women (including the so-called Christians) who could not control their tongues.

Some churches and denominations have been ruined and brought unto desolation as a result of the practice by some of the members who engage in idle chatter, gossip, rumours, speculations, tale bearing, mud slinging, character assassination, exaggeration, lying and every other thing that is contrary to holy living and sound doctrine.

We have seen cases of some denominations, churches and Christian fellowships, that have been run down by the power of the tongue by members of the church.

Anyone who has observed and followed the history of several denominations, would have discovered that the wrong use of the tongue has opened the door for the enemy to come in and introduce disintegration and problems into those churches.

No matter how holy we profess to be, no matter how prayerful the world thinks we are, and no matter how popular we are, if we allow the tongue to run riot, we would be responsible for allowing satan an inroad into the church. I have heard .heart-rendering stories concerning men of God who once vomited fire, evangelists who once demonstrated the power of God, pastors who were once flaming ministers and Christian leaders whose name spread terror in the enemy's camp but who are no more today because the enemy has used their tongues to trap them.

The devil will allow you to cast out evil spirits, he will allow you to go into spiritual warfare, he will allow you to fight household wickedness and he will allow you to go about ministering to and delivering the oppressed as long as he knows that he can trap you through your tongue.

The tongue, therefore, is the thermometer which can be used to measure your level of spirituality. Show me a woman who has succeeded in putting her tongue under control and I will show you a spiritual woman. You cannot claim that you are holy, except you have actually succeeded in controlling your tongue. You cannot claim that you are sanctified except your tongue is sanctified. You cannot lay claim to having received the second work of grace if your tongue has not been sanctified. A sanctified tongue is an index of personal inner holiness.

If we were to decide to keep a track of your life, we shall simply decide to watch how you speak, the kinds of words that come out from your tongue, and the spirit behind those words. The tongue is the greatest revealer of your level of spirituality and holiness. Nobody can claim that he or she is holy if the tongue brings out rotten, ungodly, unedifying, unwholesome, and untrue words.

Christians who exaggerate, backbite, talk excessively, spread untrue stories, run other people down, use abusive language and speak corrupt and unholy words have not even started the kindergarten class in the school of holiness.

Holiness is not determined by age. A pastor may be as old as Methuselah and he may not know what it means to be holy before the Almighty. It becomes clear, therefore, that the words of Jesus are true:

> **For I say unto you, That except your righteousness shall exceed the righteousness of the scribes and Pharisees, ye shall in no case enter into the kingdom of heaven (Matt 5:20).**

To be precise, you have not discovered what it means

to be holy until you know how to possess a holy tongue.

The Bible makes it very clear that if any man thinks that he is religious but fails to bridle or control his tongue, his religion is vain, empty and useless. God does not look at the situation the way we look at it. If God says that somebody's religion is vain, it is really true. It is crystal clear that if anybody's religion is vain, that person will surely end his or her life in hell fire.

> For he that will love life, and see good days, let him refrain his tongue from evil, and his lips that they speak no guile: (1 Pet 3:10).

This passage is self-explanatory. If anyone wants to live a godly life, such a person must avoid the wrong use of the tongue. We are also given another command in the Scriptures:

> Let no corrupt communication proceed out of your mouth, but that which is good to the use of edifying, that it may minister grace unto the hearers (Eph 4:29).

Corrupt communication must not come out from the mouth of a believer. A Christian must not crack dirty jokes. You must never speak words that could make you ashamed if such words were spoken to the entire congregation.

Furthermore, the Bible makes it clear that the believer must weigh his words before he speaks out.

> But I say unto you, That every idle word that men shall speak, they shall give account thereof in the day of judgment. For by thy words thou shalt be justified, and by thy words thou shalt be condemned (Matt 12:36-37).

Do you know that God is recording every word which you have spoken and God is going to use those words to either condemn or justify you. The Bible says,

> Seest thou a man that is hasty in his words? there is more hope of a fool than of him (Prov 29:20).

The Bible tells us that those who are guilty of talkativeness and hasty speech are fools.

The word of God is so serious about the way we use our tongues that a good portion of the Scripture is devoted to the problem of the tongue.

> A wholesome tongue is a tree of life: but perverseness therein is a breach in the spirit. . . . The heart of him that hath understanding seeketh knowledge: but the mouth of fools feedeth on foolishness (Prov 15:4,14).

These two verses teach us that a perverse tongue will lead to spiritual problems. We are also made to know that those who speak foolish words are classified as fools - those who lack any iota of wisdom.

One of the greatest commentaries on the human tongue can be found in Proverb 10:19-21:

In the multitude of words there wanteth not sin: but he that refraineth his lips is wise. The tongue of the just is as choice silver: the heart of the wicked is little worth. The lips of the righteous feed many: but fools die for want of wisdom.

These seven scriptures all agree on the importance of the human tongue. They are unanimous in their declaration of the fact that the human tongue is capable of bringing either death or life, success or failure and heaven or hell.

A lot of marriages would still be in place today if the husband and the wife had learnt how to control their tongues. A lot of companies would not have collapsed if the workers had learnt how to exercise control over their speech. Many churches which have collapsed would have been strong and united if some of the members had not allowed the devil to use their tongues as instruments of destruction.

There would have been no war in many countries and communities if the lips of members of those communities had been sealed together.

A lot of people would have passed their examinations, if they had not spoken careless words. A lot of people would have also lived wonderful lives if they never spoke any evil words with their tongues.

The tongue has, therefore, become the greatest source of problem to the lives of many people. The kind of life which God wants His people to live is made very clear in the book of Isaiah.

> **And an highway shall be there, and a way, and it shall be called The way of holiness; the unclean shall not pass over it; but it shall be for those: the wayfaring men, though fools, shall not err therein (Isa 35:8).**

The type of life which God has planned for us to live has been described by Isaiah as the way of holiness. Many people have wrong notions and ideas concerning the subject of holiness. Some believe that you are holy when you wear a sad face and appear melancholic.

Others think that to be holy, you must appear absolutely serious and stone-faced . Others expect those who are holy to be lily-livered and spineless. They expect such people to comport themselves as if they could not hurt a fly. There are those who have concluded that to be holy you must give people the impression that you are a perfect gentleman.

Others have concluded that holiness and courtesy are the same thing. Some people have even concluded that those who avoid trouble wherever they go are holy. However, all these ideas will pale into insignificance when you begin to study the word of God.

If you examine the lives of men and women who were certified holy in the Bible, they did not fit into the kind of mould described here. They were not weak-minded, slow, usually quiet, melancholic and sanctimonious. Rather, some of them were as tough as Elijah, as troublesome as John the Baptist and as tough-minded as the Lord Jesus Christ. Holy men of the Bible were sincere men.

The happiness of Paul the apostle was so deep that he could sing aloud in the prison. His happiness was deep and pronounced that he burst int o hilarious joy at midnight in the prison. Paul did not cut a picture of a lily-livered Christian.

Peter was not a gentle men, he was a holy trouble maker. He never allowed sleeping dogs to lie. He was always found asking questions, attempting the impossible and expressing himself in all sincerity and godly honesty. He was not a pretender, neither did he hide his inner feelings when he was in doubt concerning anything. He was holy without being hypocritical. He was sincere to the core yet he was acclaimed as a believer who received the experience of sanctification.

Some people give a wrong notion concerning themselves. Therefore, holiness is not repulsive; rather, it is attractive. It is a beautiful experience within the reach of every believer. It is not reserved for the angels, it is possible for all. Holy people are not those who are so heavenly conscious that they are no earthly good.

Uncleanness is the opposite of holiness. Therefore, a

holy person is separated from evil ways. He is separated unto God. No Christian who is careless about holiness is entitled to heaven. If you hate the message of holiness, you are on your way to hell fire. No one can enjoy the benefits of eternal life without accepting the message of holiness.

If you want to measure the degree of holiness in the life of a particular believer, you do so by the level of his sensitivity to sin. If you get to a level when you no longer feel sorry, troubled in your mind or aggrieved in the spirit, when you commit sin, you are not holy. If you no longer feel awfully sorry for sin, you are far from being holy. If you have lost your tears whenever you commit sin you are becoming a child of perdition. God is holy and He wants us to live a holy life.

A perfect man is a man who can rule his tongue and is rooted and grounded in the faith and in the knowledge of the Son of God. The influence of the tongue upon our lives is so vital and deep that the Holy Spirit wants to control the tongue. This is why we always quote this verse in the Scriptures: "They shall cast out devils and they shall speak with new tongues." If you cannot control your tongue and discard your former pattern of speaking, you have missed out on what it means to live a holy life.

Holiness itself is a very deep topic. The tongue is also a very deep topic. By the time you combine these two great topics you come up with a subject that is so important that it will determine your eternal destiny.

IMPORTANT FACTS

As we examine this important topic, five distinct interrelated facts emerge.

Who do you speak about? Are you a gossip or are you a rumour monger? Are you the type of Christian who goes about saying "Have you heard?" "Do not say I told you." If that describes you, you are surely doing some excellent job for the devil.

Of whom do you speak? Are you speaking what is correct about the person whom you are speaking about? Are you putting yourself into trouble by committing sin on a daily basis, speaking what you do not know anything about?

Some people commit abomination by speaking evil concerning children of God. Do you know that it is a terrible sin for you to criticise and spread rumour concerning somebody who is trying his best to serve God and his best does not seem to satisfy you?

To whom do you speak? Are they Christians? Are you the kind of believer who releases his secrets to the enemy? Whose company do you enjoy when you feel like talking? You must examine yourself.

A man could go right from the church to hell fire. If

you have bad friends in the church and you speak to such ungodly church members, you might buy yourself a free ticket to hell fire. The Bible says,

Be not deceived: evil communications corrupt good manners (1 Cor 15:33).

An English saying goes thus: Birds of the same feather flock together. Show me your friends and I will tell you the kind of person you are. If you are a prayer warrior, you will always associate yourself with praying people. If you love the word of God, your closest friends should be those who love the word of God.

If your best friends are worldly and sinful, you must be worldly and sinful yourself. If your best friend goes about committing abortion and using anti-pregnancy pills you must be an immoral person yourself. If you cannot quit the company of those who are sinful, it is an evidence of the fact that you are also sinful yourself.

A lot of people continue to keep ungodly friends under the pretext that they cannot abandon their childhood friends. A lot of people would not have found themselves in the present state of confusion which they are in, if not for their so-called childhood friends. It is very strange that some Christians allow unbelievers to be their best advisers. It is strange that a Christian, who is in the light, allows an unbeliever who is in darkness to advise him.

Do you speak into the air? Are you so overtaken by the spirit of talkativeness that you can speak to yourself when nobody is around? Such people need deliverance.

How do you speak? What kind of spirit is behind the word which you speak? Does your speech show that the Holy Spirit is in you? How do you use your tongue? Do you speak when you are supposed to be silent? Do you speak when you are supposed to be praying?

When do you speak? Do you speak whenever your brain tells you to speak? Do you ever ask the Holy Spirit to tell you if you must speak?

Where do you speak? Do you speak where the presence of God is not found? Do you speak in the company of the ungodly? Do you speak where the flesh is ruling? Where do you speak?

The tongue is a very powerful instrument that must be used with an extreme care and caution, because death and life are in its power. If you lose control over your tongue you have lost control over your life.

Somebody came to me some years ago saying, "Doctor, my husband said I should pack out of the house. Please, come and intervene between the two of us." I decided to follow her so I could talk with the husband. As we approached their house we saw the husband coming towards us. The woman opened her month and said "Dr., that is him crawling like a snake."

I asked her, "Madam, what are you saying?" I could not believe my ears.

This was a woman who had told me lots of terrible things about her husband. If you heard what she said and you were not a child of God, you would almost feel like cutting the man into pieces with a cutlass. I simply told the woman; "I am no longer ready to talk to your husband. Neither am I ready to hear anything from you. What you have just said here has shown me that you are a trouble maker."

The key to a beautiful life is to regulate and control your tongue. A Christian cannot accomplish much in the service of God if he does not know how to control his tongue. You must make a decision today to tame your tongue.

When God created man in the beginning, He endowed him with lots of power. Most of the power which God endowed us with is still with us today. For example, we still have the power of imagination and the power of exercising domination over the animals of the forest and other creatures, and the power of the spoken word. Of all these powers the greatest is the power of the spoken word. Many, today, are under bondage because of their inability to control the tongue. Many tongues are under serious bondage.

James 3:2-13 says:

For in many things we offend all. If any man offend not in word, the same is a perfect man, and able also to bridle the whole body. Behold, we put bits in the horses' mouths, that they may obey us; and we turn about their whole body. Behold also the ships, which though they be so great, and are driven of fierce winds, yet are they turned about with a very small helm, whithersoever the governor listeth. Even so the tongue is a little member, and boasteth great things. Behold, how great a matter a little fire kindleth! And the tongue is a fire, a world of iniquity: so is the tongue among our members, that it defileth the whole body, and setteth on fire the course of nature; and it is set on fire of hell. For every kind of beasts, and of birds, and of serpents, and of things in the sea, is tamed, and hath been tamed of mankind: But the tongue can no man tame; it is an unruly evil, full of deadly poison. Therewith bless we God, even the Father; and therewith curse we men, which are made after the similitude of God. Out of the same mouth proceedeth blessing and cursing. My brethren, these things ought not so to be. Doth a fountain send forth at the same place sweet water and bitter? Can the fig tree, my brethren, bear olive berries? either a vine, figs? so can no fountain both yield salt water and fresh. Who is a wise man and endued with knowledge among you? let him shew out of a good conversation his works with meekness of wisdom.

The tongue is one of the smallest members of the human body, yet it can set the whole body ablaze. It has destroyed individuals, communities, families and nations.

I read a cartoon the other day. There was a caption underneath the picture of a soldier who was holding a microphone. The caption reads, "Old men declare wars, and young men fight them." This shows us that those who actually declare wars do not fight them. Wars are declared by a few people who are privileged to hold positions of authority.

The tongue is a dangerous member of the body. I have said time and again that God gave us two eyes, two nostrils and two ears, but He gave us only one mouth because He knows that men and women are likely to misuse the tongue. Many of us find it very easy to speak all kinds of words.

The tongue can be used to serve the devil while it can also be used to serve God. It is one of the most effective passports to hell fire.

If you cannot control the tongue it will control you. Many lives were held together and everything was going on until a time came when their tongues decided to go to the north while the rest of the members of the body went the south. That is an evidence of internal and external confusion.

Let us look at the life of Zechariah, an Old Testament priest who went to the temple to perform his duties as a servant of God. An angel appeared to him bringing good news unto him from the Almighty. However, Zechariah decided to allow his mouth to run loose and put him into trouble. He was busy at the altar in the holy of holies serving the Lord. The holy of holies was a secret place which only the high priest could enter once in a year. It was so fearful that a chain was always tied around the waist of the high priest. Some bells were tied around his waist so that those who are outside the holy of holies could detect whether he was still alive or had died. That was how fearful it was to enter the holy place in those days.

The angel appeared to Zechariah and brought him wonderful news from the throne of the Almighty. However, the man, Zechariah, decided to doubt the prophetic words which the angel brought to him. The angel was unhappy with him and pronounced that it was going to be done, while Zechariah was to be dumb until it was done. If he had not been denied of the power of speech he would have talked himself out of the miracle. God had to make him dumb to help him preserve the miracle.

Do you know that there are people with demons in their tongues? Some people's tongues are so powerful that they operate independent of the other parts of their bodies. The tongue has, therefore, put many people in trouble. It becomes clear, therefore, that if you can control your tongue, you will be able to control other parts of the body. If your tongue is under satanic influence, it will speak evil words. On the hand, if your tongue is under divine influence it will speak godly words. Your life is sharpened and controlled by the type of words which you speak.

Let me make it clear once again; what is happening in your life right now is a direct result of what you have been speaking concerning yourself in the time past. What you are speaking today will also affect your future.

There is nothing so great or powerful that the tongue cannot influence. It is unfortunate that the children of the devil understand the power of the tongue. They know how to make use of the tongue to manipulate the destiny of men and women.

I witnessed a very strange experience many years ago. The incident took place at a popular bus-stop in Lagos, Nigeria. A cow suddenly broke loose from a herd of cows and there was pandemonium everywhere. Nobody was able to control the cow. Many traders and business people abandoned their premises because they feared being knocked down by the cow. Vehicles were packed, motorcyclists and riders kept a safe distance from the cow.

Nobody knew what to do until a bus attendant, popularly called bus conductor, came down from the bus and went straight to the direction of the cow and began to speak to the cow. Everybody was held spell-bound. To the surprise of everyone of us, the cow seemed to be hearing what the young man was saying. At last, the young man commanded the cow to sit down. The cow sat down quietly as if it was not the same cow that had caused a commotion a few moments earlier.

That is an example of how the children of the devil have mastered the power of the spoken word. How was he able to speak the language that the cow understands? How did he speak words which had some kind of strange authority which could calm an unmanageable cow? He had discovered the evil power which resided in the tongue. That young man must have completely given himself over to the devil to be able to tame an unruly cow. It is a case of a demon fighting another demon. Of course, the more powerful one would win.

I also witnessed another event which made me to know that the children of the devil seem to have specialised in discovering and utilisting the power of the tongue. A group of armed robbers were tied to the stakes ready for execution. A priest was brought to enable the armed robbers say their last prayers before they would be silenced forever through the gun. The armed robbers were six in number. As soon as the first round of gunshots were fired at them, five of them died. The sixth one was not affected by the gunshots. The soldiers emptied all their bullets on him, yet he remained alive.

The soldiers had to go back to the barracks for more bullets. They started again and they fired almost half of their bullets on him. The man kept on starring at them as if he was on a picnic. As this drama went on, an old man, who was tucked somewhere in the crowd, called the army officer who was in charge of the execution and said: "Young man, let me help you. You have tried to kill this man for more than two hours now and you have not succeeded. I have been watching the whole drama. But let me tell you the secret. Have you noticed that the armed robber has continued to chant some powerful incantation while your men were busy shooting at him? You will never be able to kill him as long as you continue to allow him to speak. If you really want to kill him, tell your boys to aim at his mouth. Once you are able to shoot his mouth he will stop chanting those incantations. Immediately he stops chanting incantations, command your boys to shoot all the other parts of his body. He will die instantly."

The armed officer thanked the old man and gave the soldiers fresh orders. As soon as they shot the armed robber's mouth and others were fired at his body, he died. That is a very good example of the power of the tongue.

The tongue is the most powerful part of human body. You cannot experience victory in life unless you know how to exercise control over your tongue. If you use your tongue negatively, you cannot expect the same tongue to have power over witches and wizards.

The tongue is so central in the life of men that God has given us a wonderful provision with which we can transform our tongues. The baptism with the Holy Spirit provides us with a divine opportunity to change our tongues. You must allow the Holy Spirit to control your tongue.

Your tongue needs deliverance because most tongues are under bondage. Many tongues need cleansing because they are dirty. Some unclean spirits have made the tongue their place of abode. Some people's tongues have been controlled and animated by the power of the flesh. That is why anyone whose tongue is not yet liberated and made holy cannot experience what it means to live a holy life.

Excessive talking, idle and careless words, gossiping, lying, being hasty in speaking, swearing and cursing and being involved in cracking dirty jokes, must be flushed out of your tongue, if you want your word to carry power before the Almighty.

The Bible says: **"If you want to see good days, you must refrain your tongue from speaking evil and your lips from guile."**

Some of us have copied the devil's vocabulary. Listen to the so-called Christians and you will hear slangs like "bread", "chick", "paddy" and other words which portray the language of the people of the world. A lot of Christians who are now born again learnt some incantations before they became born again. If you are not careful you might still speak the same words, once in a while. You must ask God to erase such demonic words from your memory through the power of the Holy Spirit.

If you speak evil with your tongue it will set the whole body on fire. Some people pray like this: "Holy Spirit, send Your fire into my life" and expect the Holy Spirit to descend upon them, they use the same tongue to abuse, curse, exaggerate and commit immorality. Can the Holy Spirit take control of such a thing? What has the Holy Spirit got to do with a dirty, immoral tongue? How can God deposit His power in your tongue when you use the same tongue to crack dirty jokes? Can God anoint the tongue of a man who has become an encyclopedia in cursing and using abusive words? That is why many people have not been able to receive the Holy Spirit. The Holy Spirit is a very clean spirit; He has no affinity with those who are living dirty lives.

Because of the state of their tongues, some people try to console themselves when they cannot receive the baptism in the Holy Spirit by saying; "It is not compulsory that I must speak in tongues. There are many other gifts in the Bible."

Paul, the apostle said, "I thank my God that I speak

in tongues more than ye all." If Paul could speak in tongues what excuses do you have? You must not deceive yourself. You must deal with the problem of the tongue. You must release your tongue from the control and domination of evil spirits.

If the tongues of many people can receive transformation, it means they will begin to experience wonderful blessings from the Almighty. Many people have gone into bondage through their lips. Before they became born again, some people were fond of sharing cigarettes and sweets with just anybody, not knowing if they were sharing things with people who dedicated their tongues to the devil. Others eat sacrifices when they were not born again, such people have serious problems now.

To deal with such problems, you must receive the touch of God on your tongue and let God do something new in your life. Do you know that if you make up your mind that you are not going to allow evil words to come off your lips for one week, you will experience wonderful miracles. If you can make up your mind that starting from today, you will not speak a single negative word about your job, your family, your health and your future, and you do that for one week you will be shocked by the kind of miracle which will happen to you. But I wonder how many can do that, since most people are under a serious demonic influence.

If your words are dominated by doubt you will be conquered by negative circumstances. If you speak about failure all the time you will fail. If you are always talking about weakness, you will become weak. If you talk about poverty and lack, poverty will move into your territory and dominate your life. If you keep on expressing fear, fear will grip your heart.

Isa. 6:1-7 says:

> In the year that king Uzziah died I saw also the Lord sitting upon a throne, high and lifted up, and his train filled the temple. Above it stood the seraphims: each one had six wings; with twain he covered his face, and with twain he covered his feet, and with twain he did fly. And one cried unto another, and said, Holy, holy, holy, is the LORD of hosts: the whole earth is full of his glory. And the posts of the door moved at the voice of him that cried, and the house was filled with smoke. Then said I, Woe is me! for I am undone; because I am a man of unclean lips, and I dwell in the midst of a people of unclean lips: for mine eyes have seen the King, the LORD of hosts. Then flew one of the seraphims unto me, having a live coal in his hand, which he had taken with the tongs from off the altar: And he laid it upon my mouth, and said, Lo, this hath touched thy lips; and thine iniquity is taken away, and thy sin purged.

This passage reveals a lot about the holiness of God and the impact it can make on your life. It also reveals the greatest problems of many church-goers. We are made to know that many church-goers are yet to know the Lord. A lot of Christians who have spent several years in the church are yet to have an unforgettable encounter with the Lord. Although they know so much about the church, they know nothing about the Lord.

Some members of the church have had encounters with pastors, general overseers, miracles, well-thought-out sermons and oratory, but they are yet to find God. Your priority changes the moment you have an encounter with the Lord; you will also see yourself the way you really are. My prayer for you, as you continue to read the pages of this book, is that you have a new life-transforming encounter with the Lord. Nobody will need to preach several sermons to you before you begin to live for the glory of God.

One thing we all need, which most believers lack, is to receive a touch of fire from the hand of Almighty God. Immediately Isaiah identified his problems and owned up to his inadequacy, God visited him. A single touch from the Lord turned Isaiah's life around. He became the greatest prophet in the Old Testament. For example, Isaiah predicted a great proportion of the events in the life and ministry of the Lord Jesus Christ. He couldn't make those prophetic declarations until the fire of God fell upon his tongue. When the fire of God fell upon Isaiah, he was dramatically transformed. The fire of God fell upon him and left him broken, renewed and transformed. The touch of the Lord burnt off every dirt and rubbish from his life.

The reason many lives continue to remain under bondage can be traced to the fact that they are yet to have a genuine encounter with the Lord. The reason many people visit several prayer houses, churches and deliverance ministries without experiencing any change in their lives can be traced to the fact that they have not experienced the fire of God in their lives. Those who have received the touch of fire discover that their bonds have been broken.

More than any other thing, you need the baptism of fire. You need the fire of God to purge you and sweep away every form of rubbish from your life. If we were to go by the perfect plan of God for our lives, we are supposed to encounter the fire of God the very day we gave our lives to Christ. The baptism of fire should come upon you the day you receive the baptism of the Holy Spirit.

Many have not experienced the fire of God because of their failure to allow God to purge and set them on fire. The Holy Spirit can not force anybody. It is unfortunate that some people are scared of what will likely happen to them if the fire of God should come upon their lives.

Why are you afraid of the fire of the Holy Spirit? Do you prefer to remain under bondage? Do you know that your fears are unfounded? What do you expect? Why are you afraid of being useful in the hand of God? Do you know that I was like that before? I never knew that God could use me in this magnitude.

How did it happen? I simply surrendered myself to Him. I remember a particular man who was making jest of me saying that I was too serious with God. I was shocked later when I came across him carrying a Bible, that was two times bigger than mine, in spite of the fact that he was formerly a Muslim.

The reason many lives are cold and ineffective in the hand of God can be traced to the fact that they are yet to have an encounter with the fire of the Holy Spirit. You need to have a fresh a encounter with God.

God sent tongues of fire upon the apostles. Why did God send the Holy Spirit to the apostles in the form of fire? It is because of the power of the tongue and because the fire of the Holy Spirit finds expression in the tongue. We need the fire of the Holy Spirit today.

The Bible tells us that John the Baptist was filled with the Holy Spirit from his mother's womb. Bible scholars tell us that, more people became born again through the ministry of John the Baptist than through the ministry of his contemporaries. When Jesus was asked a question concerning John the Baptist, the Lord simply declared that John was more than a prophet. If you study the words of John the Baptist, you will discover that he preached very tough messages. He received tongues of fire.

Let the fire of God fall upon your tongue today and your life will no longer be the same.

PRAYER POINTS

1. Father Lord, soak me in the fire of the Holy Ghost, in the name of Jesus.

2. O Lord, do unto me what You did to Isaiah.

The tongue of power

Prophet Isaiah is one of the most anointed prophets in the Old Testament. He had an encounter with God, which transformed his life.

The transformation of Isaiah's tongue is one of the most important things that ever happened to him. God used him to bring the important message of the coming of the Messiah to mankind. God touched his tongue which was the channel of the divine message.

Isa. 6:1-4 says:

> In the year that king Uzziah died I saw also the Lord sitting upon a throne, high and lifted up, and his train filled the temple. Above it stood the seraphims: each one had six wings; with twain he covered his face, and with twain he covered his feet, and with twain he did fly. And one cried unto another, and said, Holy, holy, holy, is the LORD of hosts: the whole earth is full of his glory. And the posts of the door moved at the voice of him that cried, and the house was filled with smoke.

The passage has a lot to say concerning what it means to have an encounter with God. One thing stands out clearly here. When you see the Lord, something must happen to you. Any genuine encounter with the Lord must remain unforgettable in your memory. The picture of a real encounter with God remains with you wherever you go and throughout the days of your life.

What we need today is an unforgettable encounter with the Almighty. We need to understand that it is possible to spend several years in the church without having a single encounter with God. It is also possible to get involved with all facets of Christian service without having a face-to-face encounter with God.

The divine encounter will be made real to you if you seek the Lord with all your heart. The moment you have that encounter your life will change. Situations that had appeared confusing and hopeless will be turned around by God.

The reason the problems of many people have remained resistant to prayer can be traced to lack of a decisive encounter with God. If that describes your situation, what you need is a divine encounter.

Isa. 6:5 says:

Then said I, Woe is me! for I am undone; because I am a man of unclean lips, and I dwell in the midst of a people of unclean lips: for mine eyes have seen the King, the LORD of hosts.

Another lesson which we ought to learn from Isaiah's experience is that a divine encounter will reveal your true spiritual condition to you. When you see the Lord, nobody needs to tell you what your spiritual stand looks like. You will be able to face reality without deceiving yourself. You will see yourself the way you really are. You wouldn't need a preacher to tell you where you are missing the mark.

A single encounter with God will make you to see yourself in the light of the word of God. You will discover whether you are a glorified hypocrite. You will see yourself plainly when you see the Lord.

Isa. 6:6-8 says:

> **Then flew one of the seraphims unto me, having a live coal in his hand, which he had taken with the tongs from off the altar: And he laid it upon my mouth, and said, Lo, this hath touched thy lips; and thine iniquity is taken away, and thy sin purged. Also I heard the voice of the Lord, saying, Whom shall I send, and who will go for us? Then said I, Here am I; send me.**

Isaiah had a very close encounter with God. He came face to face with the holy God. The Bible makes us to understand that God is holy and His presence is enveloped with holiness in its superlative form.

Isaiah had been ministering in the house of God and in the midst of the people of God. If he were to compare himself with the people, he would have said that he was very much above average. He was so righteous in the eyes of the people that his calling to the ministry and the enviable position which he occupied, as well as his spiritual stature, made him to look larger than life.

It is very easy, for men and women who minister in the house of God to be so highly exalted, that their faults are no longer seen by those who are close to them. It is also possible they are so anointed, that people will begin to look at them as if they are no longer human. The situation becomes worse, when such people are no longer ready to look at their true spiritual condition and face the reality. Many so-called ministers have missed the mark because they felt elevated above their measure.

Isaiah, perhaps, was the best example of godliness in his days. He was almost worshipped by the people who surrounded him. They almost elevated him to the rank of divinity. It is possible that Isaiah enjoyed the super status before he was brought to the sanctuary, where the Lord ran him through a tough spiritual diagnosis. Isaiah was so baffled by what he saw that he cried out, "Woe is me for I am undone. For I am a man of unclean lips and I dwell in the midst of unclean people." God had to take him away from the crowd before he could see the glory of God and his personal depravity and shortcoming.

I don't know how busy you are, and I don't know if you have ever taken the time to run yourself through a spiritual check-up in the presence of God. What we often lose sight of is, the fact that we are the best among a group of people, does not mean that we have attained a position of success.

I wonder what would have happened to Isaiah if he did not have that encounter with God. What do you think would have happened to Isaiah if he had died as a man of unclean lips? His experience shows us that a popular minister or a respected man of God, who happens to be in high demand among men, may miss the mark and become unacceptable to God.

What Isaiah said concerning himself, shows us that he was a man of unclean lips, unsafe of all the divine messages which he had delivered to the children of Israel. Before that time, Isaiah must have stood up gallantly beating his chest and speaking with an air of success and acceptability. The brief moment he spent in the presence of God granted him the opportunity of receiving a divine X-ray of his spiritual condition. The result of the X-ray, was so appealing that he had to pronounce woe upon himself.

Many of our modern-day ministers are quite different from Isaiah. If you correct a pastor and challenge him to shape up spiritually, he will look for a hundred and one reasons to cover up his shortcomings. How many ministers and church workers can own up to their spiritual shortcomings and say, "Woe unto me for I am undone?" How many members of the choir are ready to say that they are men and women of unclean lips even when they render beautiful songs in the house of God? How many teachers and pastors are ready to agree with heaven's verdict concerning their lives?

Isaiah accepted his personal problem and he also recognized the fact that the people to whom he ministered were having some sort of negative impact upon his life.

The easiest route to hell fire is sometimes found in the church. It can be very easy for a preacher to miss heaven. It is very simple for a man of God who receives praises and accolades from the congregation to miss the track. Isaiah was probably too busy to examine his spiritual state. He did not know that his life was stinking to the nostril of God, as he was busy serving the people. He was awake to the realisation of the ugly state of affairs in his life when his eyes were opened to see the glory of the Lord. Immediately Isaiah saw the Lord, the problem with his life was brought into the open. He discovered for the first time in his life that his lips were polluted and his tongue was contaminated. Therefore, his words carried no power.

KING UZZIAH

The incident under consideration in this chapter took place around 742 B.C. Isaiah happened to be a middle-aged man around that time. He had an encounter with God while the evening sacrifice was taking place in the church. The reigning monarch at that time was Uzziah the king of Judah.

Uzziah, one of the most prominent kings in the ancient kingdom had just died. The Bible makes it very clear that every good thing that happened in the life of Isaiah took place after the death of king Uzziah. Who was king Uzziah? Let us examine 2 Chron. 26:1-5,

Then all the people of Judah took Uzziah, who was sixteen years old, and made him king in the room of his father Amaziah. He built Eloth, and restored it to Judah, after that the king slept with his fathers. Sixteen years old was Uzziah when he began to reign, and he reigned fifty and two years in Jerusalem. His mother's name also was Jecoliah of Jerusalem. And he did that which was right in the sight of the LORD, according to all that his father Amaziah did. And he sought God in the days of Zechariah, who had understanding in the visions of God: and as long as he sought the LORD, God made him to prosper.

Let us look at verse 15:

And he made in Jerusalem engines, invented by cunning men, to be on the towers and upon the bulwarks, to shoot arrows and great stones withal. And his name spread far abroad; for he was marvellously helped, till he was strong.

I want you to take a particular notice of verses 16-23

But when he was strong, his heart was lifted up to

his destruction: for he transgressed against the LORD his God, and went into the temple of the LORD to burn incense upon the altar of incense. And Azariah the priest went in after him, and with him fourscore priests of the LORD, that were valiant men: And they withstood Uzziah the king, and said unto him, It appertaineth not unto thee, Uzziah, to burn incense unto the LORD, but to the priests the sons of Aaron, that are consecrated to burn incense: go out of the sanctuary; for thou hast trespassed; neither shall it be for thine honour from the LORD God. Then Uzziah was wroth, and had a censer in his hand to burn incense: and while he was wroth with the priests, the leprosy even rose up in his forehead before the priests in the house of the LORD, from beside the incense altar. And Azariah the chief priest, and all the priests, looked upon him, and, behold, he was leprous in his forehead, and they thrust him out from thence; yea, himself hasted also to go out, because the LORD had smitten him. And Uzziah the king was a leper unto the day of his death, and dwelt in a several house, being a leper; for he was cut off from the house of the LORD: and Jotham his son was over the king's house, judging the people of the land. Now the rest of the acts of Uzziah, first and last, did Isaiah the prophet, the son of Amoz, write. So Uzziah slept with his fathers, and they buried him with his fathers in the field of the burial which belonged to the kings; for they said, He is a leper: and Jotham his son reigned in his stead.

Uzziah performed better than most of the kings who lived in his days but his strength made him proud. His reign was beneficial, physically, to the entire nation. But money and splendour corrupted the hearts of the people.

Those who lived in the days of Isaiah had departed from the Lord. The people who Isaiah ministered to had completely forgotten that they were called to be a holy nation. They were no longer living their lives in conformity with the word of God. They were no longer trusting in God to protect them and provide for their needs. They were conforming to the ungodly influence, which surrounded them. Their belly and their ears had become heavy. They were unable to speak the word of the Lord. They could not even hear what the Lord was saying to them. They had actually departed from the Lord. Both Isaiah and the people whom he was ministering to, were backsliding totally.

That was his spiritual state, before he saw the Lord. That was how he had a once-and-for-all encounter which transformed his life. Therefore, if you want to experience a change of life and if you want your tongue to carry the power of God, you must have an encounter with God, who is the giver of power. If you fail to have an encounter with God and you go about praying that the power of God should fall upon your tongue, nothing will happen to you.

The Bible says "Death and life are in the power of the tongue" This passage shows that your tongue will either carry power or it will carry weakness. Your tongue will either be a carrier of faith and an encouragement, or it will be a carrier of discouragement or despair. Your tongue can carry discouragement, sickness and failure. However, the kind of tongue, which God wants us to have, is the tongue that carries power.

I normally get challenged when I read about children of the devil who sleep at the graveyard for 201 days just because they are searching for power. Children of the devil also discipline themselves and fast because they are looking for power. Those who belong to the devil memorise incantations while children of God find it difficult to memorise the word of God.

STEPS TO RECEIVE POWER

Divine encounter - The unclean lip must be dealt with, but that can only take place when you have an encounter with the one who gives power.

Fire in your tongue - The second step, which you must take to possess the tongue of power, is to allow God drop His coal of fire upon your tongue. That experience will purge your sins and wipe away your iniquity. Unless you allow God to deal with your tongue, you will end up being like the seven sons of Sceva, who tried to cast out evil spirits without having any encounter with God. You must allow God to deal with your tongue. You must allow the fire of God to fall upon it.

The moment you have a decisive encounter with God,

which results in the subjection of your tongue under the fire of the Holy Spirit, you will no longer be the same again.

Death to Uzziah. The third step, which you must take, is that your 'Uzziah must die'. What is your Uzziah? Simply put, it is that which blocks you from seeing God, that which prevents you from experiencing divine revelation.

Whatever has made you so comfortable that you no longer desire to pray is your Uzziah. What keeps you so busy that you have no time for heartfelt praying is your Uzziah. That Uzziah must die.

Why don't you make this prayer statement:

My Uzziah must die today, in the name of Jesus.

As long as your Uzziah is alive you cannot possess the tongue of power. Two kings, we all know, cannot sit on the same throne. As long as the throne of your life is occupied by king Uzziah, God cannot anoint your tongue with power. It is of no use to go about saying, "I am going to reign with Christ one of these days," when you are living under bondage. It is also not reasonable to say that you belong to Christ, when you are having sex in the dream every night. You cannot say that you truly belong to Christ, when you are being pursued by masquerades in your dream every night. You cannot say that you are a true believer when you grow wings and fly in the dream every night.

Those experiences are far away from God's plan for your life. What other things does Uzziah stand for? King Uzziah is a symbol of pride and self-confidence. Isaiah did not amount to anything before God until king Uzziah died. When you take these steps you are then ready to allow God to put his coals of fire upon your tongue. You will also be ready to allow Him to destroy those things which are limiting God's power in your life.

You must allow the Holy Spirit to possess your life. The Bible says, "Walk in the spirit and ye shall not fulfil the desires of the flesh." You must lay down all your weapons of rebellion and yield the steering of your life to the control of the Holy Spirit. Once you have taken that step, you then go ahead to pray that God should purge your life.

Your tongue is either dead or alive. Your tongue is either an instrument of glorification or a weapon of bondage. You need a close encounter with God today. Your Uzziah must die. Open your heart to the Lord. Let God deal with every sin of malice, pride, fornication, adultery and backbiting, lying and other evidences of the fact that the totality of your life is not yet yielded to the Lord.

Be sincere with yourself. Allow the Lord to do a work in your life. Let the Lord transform your tongue today.

8

The madness of the mind

The Bible gives us a shocking revelation in the book of Ecclesiastes:

> **This is an evil among all things that are done under the sun, that there is one event unto all: yea, also the heart of the sons of men is full of evil, and madness is in their heart while they live, and after that they go to the dead (Eccl 9:3).**

There is an inseparable link between the mind and the tongue. The tongue speaks out what is stored in the mind. A good heart will produce wholesome words. When the mind is sick, the whole body becomes unmanageable. That is why the Bible screams out:

> **Keep thy heart with all diligence; for out of it are the issues of life (Prov 4:23).**

Here, the Bible enjoins every believer to protect the mind and keep it away from all evil influences.

Why is the heart so important that it occupies a central place in the lives of all mortals? The heart or the mind is the only link which we have with God. We are made alive unto God through our minds. We perceive the truth of the Scriptures with our hearts and we make all our efforts towards worshipping God through the human mind. That is why the Bible commands that:

And thou shalt love the Lord thy God with all thy heart, and with all thy soul, and with all thy mind, and with all thy strength: this is the first commandment (Mark 12:30).

We see in this command the importance of the mind. That is why it is important to keep the mind in a good condition. If anything goes wrong with the mind, the totality of your life will be turned upside down.

On the other hand, if your mind is wholesome, your life will also be whole. You need to understand that wrong words are spoken when the heart or the mind is under the control of the devil. A lot of people have wondered why most of the words which men speak in the society today are evil words. We do not need to go too far before we understand the reason.

The Bible makes it very clear that the heart of man is full of evil and madness is lodged within the heart of men and women. Many people cannot control the words they speak because of the madness of the mind. We need the opening of our eyes of understanding to understand what the madness of the mind is all about.

When the phrase, 'the madness of the mind' is used, many people begin to think about the minds of men and women. There are various levels of madness. There are low levels of madness and there are high levels of madness. There are different levels or degree of madness.

What comes to your mind when you see a male prophet bathing a lady by the side of the river? That is an example of low level of madness.

Somebody loses his temper and rages violently. That is another example of elementary madness.

Or how can you explain the fact that the body of an angry man continues to vibrate even after the quarrel is over. That is a manifestation of madness.

A lot of things are happening today. We sometimes see some ladies who become false prophets and go about ringing bells when the totality of their body is bleached.

I had an experience when I was in a secondary school several years ago. There was a particular preacher who came to the bus-stop early in the morning and preached to a little crowd who were trying to jump into the buses. I never saw a single person who waited behind to listen to him. Although he was normal, he appeared not to be in control of his mind. If his mind was wholesome he would have realised that it did not make any sense to preach when nobody was listening.

I had a very troublesome classmate who decided to tell the elderly man to think of a better way of preaching the gospel. I decided to follow him and we headed straight to the elderly preacher. "Papa, you appear to have been wasting your time. Why do you stand at this bus-stop preaching when no one is listening to you? Why don't you preach to them when they are through with their daily duties or why don't you go to a place where you can find people who are ready to listen to you?"

The elderly man said, "Thank you, my son. That is very thoughtful of you. Let me help you by giving you some portion of the Psalms. Use the portions for your exams and you will always come out in flying colours."

We were surprised, to find the same preacher at the same bus-stop the next day preaching to the same people who were so much in a hurry that they found it difficult to wait and listen for a minute. This was a type of madness.

There are many mad people on the streets today, who are well dressed and intelligent. Many of them appear normal on the surface but they are not well adjusted emotionally. There is partial madness and there is complete madness. When somebody runs mad (whether it is partial or complete) it means that he has lost all forms of inhibitions. That is exactly what happens to those who are drunk. They lose every sense of decency and moral correctness. Let us, therefore, look at the characteristics of madness of the mind.

The mind is the greatest battle field. If your mind is already captured there is no battle which you can fight. A lot of people who go from one hospital to another will be healed if they can pray about the healing of the mind. Many people do not know that the problems which they have grappled with for several years emanated from the mind. The best thing to do, therefore, is to know how to deal with the problem of the mind. There will be less problems and sicknesses in the society if the problems of the mind are dealt with.

THE SYMPTOMS OF MADNESS OF THE MIND

What then are the symptoms of the madness of the mind?

Worry - It is spiritual madness for anyone to sit down and extol God's sufficient grace one moment and go ahead to lament his problems in life the next moment. The contradiction which are expressed by you shows that you are suffering from madness of the mind. Those who worry and are suffering from the madness of the mind must address this serious issue. If you have this kind of problem you must deal with it seriously.

Failure to do so may lead you into more serious problems. Your mind may become a battle zone. You might even go into total backsliding from that stage. Worry and anxiety are among our greatest problems today. I get close to 500 letters a week from those who believe that their matters require an urgent attention.

I have discovered that a good number of the people who write such letters, only need someone to either talk with or listen to them. If you allow the devil to reduce you to a worry bag he will bring several other problems into your life.

Feeling that one is completely useless - Some people write themselves off completely by concluding that they are good for nothing and useless. Such people go about complaining: "What kind of life is this? Everything is upside down." Such people are quick to say, "I've tried almost everything but nothing has ever worked. I tried marriage and it failed. I tried my profession and it is not working. Maybe, I should end it all."

After making such a statement the devil will make several suggestions. The devil will speak to you saying, "You can jump down from a very high bridge or hang yourself with a rope. You can also drink poison. That would be a very quick way of ending everything." If you feel that your life is totally useless, you will be tired of life itself.

Depression - Depression is one of the most terrible problems that can plague the human heart. The Bible calls it 'the spirit of heaviness'. There is a heavy load on the minds of those who are going through moments of depression. Some people become so depressed that they do not want to talk to anybody.

Some people become so depressed that they lock themselves up in a room for several days.

Some special demons move into the life of their victim to turn him or her to a wreck.

I know a man who experienced such an attack. He came back to Nigeria from England after finishing his degree. He got a good job and was full of great expectations. Having studied in England, he expected things to go on perfectly. Things became worse because he was also a stickler for perfection, punctuality and excellence. He was employed as a manager of a flourishing company. Hardly had he started the job than the entire company turned upside down. The official resumption time was 7.30 a.m. If anyone resumed after 7.30 a.m. such a person would be disciplined. He gave lots of queries to the people for coming a minute or two late to the office.

The people who were given queries began to deal with him in their own kinds of ways. Things became so bad that the chairman of the company had to call him and said: "Manager, what is this company being turned into? We've been running the company before you came. Why don't you take it easy? This is not England. This is

Nigeria."

The man refused to listen to the chairman. That was how he was given a letter of termination of appointment. He couldn't get another job for a very long time. He became so depressed that he decided to lock himself up and he refused to talk to anyone. He went into what can be called the madness of the mind.

High mindedness - A lot of people are so high-minded that they live in the world of fantasy. They mind high things and esteem themselves above measure. They don't want to start at the lower level. They want to do what will attract the attention of everyone. The devil uses high mindedness against people. High mindedness will make you to struggle for what you can achieve with ease. Even if God sets a table before you, high mindedness will make you to push it away.

Some people go about saying, "I'm going to use the latest brand of Mercedes to do my wedding." Some others would even tell us, "I want to do my wedding in an airplane." That is a typical example of high mindedness. What has an airplane got to do with marriage? What impact will the latest brand of Mercedes have on your marriage? Some people would say, "The Head of State will be the chairman of my wedding reception." That is how high-mindedness can take its victims.

High-mindedness has made many people to lose their peace. High-mindedness will lead you into unreasonable actions. It would make it obvious to people that you are a victim of the madness of the mind.

Sadness - There is a kind of sadness that is not ordinary. Some people become sad for no just reason. They are sad before they go to bed at night and they wake up early in the morning with terrible sad feelings. It is an evidence of the fact that the mind is mad.

Hopelessness - Many people feel that the situation around them is completely hopeless. That is another symptom of madness of the mind

Guilt - A lot of people feel guilty for what does not really exist. You commit a sin 15 years ago and God has forgiven you. Instead of accepting God's forgiveness, you go about harassing yourself over what God no longer remembers. How long will you allow the guilt of what God has cast into the sea of forgetfulness to keep haunting you?

The guilt which many people are going through today does not emanate from the devil - the accuser of the brethren. It is self-made. The guilt, which you have allowed to hold your mind, emanates from your own heart, not from the devil.

Dwelling in the past - Those who dwell in the past do not have a wholesome mind. Some people spend their lives living in the distant past. Why must you worry about yesterday? Yesterday is gone forever. That is a symptom of the madness of the mind. You must not worry about previous situations and problems since you cannot go back to the past.

Unnecessary agitation - A lot of people easily get agitated by situations when they are supposed to maintain control over such situations.

Inability to concentrate - A lot of people cannot control their minds. They cannot focus their hearts on a single subject or matter. They carry the Bible and they try to pray at the same time. They vacillate over matters and situations without being able to lay hold on one.

Lack of confidence - This is also a symptom of madness of the mind. People who fall into lack of self-confidence feel timid and are not able to face anything without feeling inferior.

Anger - This is another evidence of the madness of the mind.

Fear of death - Many people spend everyday thinking that they may die. That is another symptom of madness of the mind.

Lack of motivation - This category of people face life situations without any iota of interest or excitement.

Addiction to weeping - There are people who are easily moved to tears whenever a little thing happens to them. They live as if they are addicted to crying. That is another instance of the madness of the mind.

Feeling of isolation - Talk to some people and they will give you the impression that everyone on earth is against them. That is a clear example of the sickness of the mind. Why must you allow that kind of feeling to bother you? Even if everyone on earth is against you, the fact that God is standing by your side makes you more than a conqueror.

The human mind is the greatest vagabond in the universe. You might be in a particular place while your mind is thousands of miles away. If you refuse to put that kind of vagabond condition of the mind under control, it will eventually lead you into serious problems.

It is unfortunate, that what psychiatric hospitals do, is to collect house rents when the rooms of people's lives are already hired out. Some people's mind have also been converted to concrete slabs by the devil. They cannot make any progress in life.

Many minds are also abodes of complex cobwebs. Such people are fond of running away from God whenever God is trying to reach out to them. The only thing that can bring progress into their lives is change. Unfortunately, they hate changes. They want things to continue the same way they have been. Many people who claim that they have an open minds are only deceiving themselves. Their minds are as closed as any human mind can be. All they have is a blank space.

There is no free thinker anywhere. Jesus called a spade a spade during his earthly ministry. He denounced all the evil things which people do. Jesus is the only preacher who talked most about hell fire. Although He came to demonstrate the love of God to a lost humanity, He was the only preacher who spoke the truth concerning hell the fire.

There is nothing like a liberal mind. God gives us no room for such. If you go about saying that you have a liberal mind, you are living in self-deceit. Little minds are affected by little things. When a man's mind is really little, insignificant things hurt him.

Somebody was called a brother and he flared up. He was angry because the other fellow referred to him as a brother. He said, "Me, a brother? How can you call me brother so and so? Don't you know that I am a man of God? Don't call me brother so and so. Call me Pastor or Reverend so and so. I wont allow you to put me in the same category with other Christians. Do you know what God has deposited in my life? Don't ever make that mistake again." But why should someone get angry because he was referred to as a brother? That was an evidence of possessing a little mind. Little minds react to little things while great minds respond to great things.

Anyone who constantly thinks of himself, will end up becoming discouraged. If you centre all your thoughts on yourself you will easily get tired of yourself. Again, I want you to know that it takes a strong mind to control a wild tongue. If your mind is loose, your tongue will also run loose. If your heart is open to Satanic incursion it will soon become a dumping ground for all kinds of garbage or rubbish.

It is indeed dangerous to invite enemies into your mind. The devil will give you topics to deliberate upon. If you go to a proper school of deliverance, one of the first lessons they will teach you is that every demon has its own assignment. They will also teach you that every geographical area has a territorial spirit or a ruling demon. They will make you to understand that there is a Yoruba demon, an Hausa demon, an Igbo demon, an Urhobo demon. They will also teach you that there is something called a 'strongman' who is in charge of junior demons in the evil world. One thing which they will also teach you is that the demon of anger is the gate-keeper over the lives of men and women.

The demons of anger stand at the gate poised and dignified. He mounts the gate like an executive gateman. The moment you get angry, the demon of anger will open the gate and beckon to his other colleagues telling them that the time is right for them to come in and take control. Problems like diseases, hypertension, poverty, and demonic attacks will quickly rush in. By the time your anger subsides, they would have succeeded in taking a total control of your life. That is how problems will become resident in your life waiting for another time of momentary madness.

A sister dragged her husband to me saying: "This is the foolish man. It's because of him I have tried to book this appointment. The man opened his mouth and said: "Man of God, I am really sorry to disturb you. I decided to follow her to your office because I know that she can kill me if I did not. However, Pastor, I must tell you that I'm grateful to God for what He has used your church to do in her life. She was actually worse than this. I've continued to encourage her to keep on coming to your church because I've seen slight changes in her life."

That was what anger did in the life of that sister. I hope that does not describe your own situation. If you are in the same shoes with her you need deliverance as well as complete overhauling of your life.

A lot of people will go to hell fire if their life is not totally free, from evil influence. If you are only partially free your heart is the devil's property. That is why the Bible challenges every believer to renew his or her mind through the word of God. When you get born again, you need the word of God to clear off every old debris of your former life. As you continue to renew your mind through the word of God, you will begin to experience wonderful changes in your life.

A lot of people will go to hell fire if their life is not free from evil influence. You must be assured that the totality of your life is not the property of the devil. It becomes clear, therefore, that if you win a person's mind you have captured him. If you capture his thoughts you control him. This explains why satan fights to capture the hearts of men and women. He knows that once he takes control of the heart he has won the battle.

The Bible says:

> **But I fear, lest by any means, as the serpent beguiled Eve through his subtilty, so your minds should be corrupted from the simplicity that is in Christ (2 Cor 11:3).**

The devil aims at the human mind. His goal is to corrupt the simplicity of your mind. The devil came to Eve in the garden and manipulated her mind until she was influenced to disobey God. Satan fed Eve's mind with lots of negative information until she decided to disobey God. She doubted the word of God and believed the lies of the devil. All that happened because the devil succeeded in beguiling Eve. Her mind was corrupted from the simplicity which resided in it before the time of the fall.

What happened to Eve has happened to several other

people today. More and more people are having their minds corrupted and shifted away from the simplicity that is in Christ.

The moment that happens, the devil has succeeded in removing your feet from the solid rock. To stand on a slippery ground is to fall. I want you to lay your hand on your chest as you take this prayer point:

My mind, go back to your resting place, in the name of Jesus.

There is no doubt that you know the state of your own heart. How do you think the Lord looks at your heart at this moment? If Jesus were to come to you right now and flash the torch of His holy and high standard towards your heart, what will His verdict be? The Lord is not interested in your outward appearance; His focus is on your heart. It is possible to appear respectable and godly outwardly and be filled with wickedness internally. You may look so holy outwardly as if you could not even hurt a fly while your heart is filled with destruction, adultery, anger, worry and depression.

What you have read so far and what you continue to read in this book is for your spiritual welfare. Therefore, you must not take the great truth lightly.

SATANIC SUGGESTIONS

One thing which the devil has continued to use with great success against the minds of people is suggestions. Suggestions are generally subtle. They look very attractive when viewed at the surface level. However, most suggestions are evil. If you do not know how to counter suggestions, you will find yourself agreeing with them. You will go out of your way to do what you did not intend to do.

When evil suggestions have completely taken over your heart, you will find yourself acting in the direction of those suggestions. For example, the devil might tell you, "Don't you know how intelligent you are? Why should someone with your own kind of brain suffer poverty. Why don't you get smart and cheat on your company? You could make millions of naira that way. After all, everybody is doing it."

The devil might also tell you, "Don't you know that you are very handsome. Handsome people like you generally have a chain of girl-friends. If you continue that way, you are sure of getting married to the lady of your dream."

The devil might also tell you, "If you are a lady, what are you doing with your beauty. Why do you go about complaining that you have no money? Do you know that beautiful ladies like you generally go out with as many men as possible? That's how they make their money. Don't be left out. Go out. Have a good time and make your own money too."

All these are satanic suggestions. The devil is fond of giving smart suggestions. If somebody gives you an amount of money, the devil will be on hand to offer a suggestion saying, "Why don't you remove some amount of money and go back to the person telling him that the money given to you was not complete? Talk to him as if you really mean what you are saying. If you do that you will make some money." That is another smart suggestion.

All these suggestions may lead you into all kind of devilish practices.

Somebody entered a bus and found ₦100 on the seat. He quickly grabbed the money and felt like asking the commuters in the bus: "Who is the owner of this money?" The devil gave him a suggestion, "If you make such an announcement, you will miss the money. A smart fellow will claim that he or she is the owner." He accepted the satanic suggestion and went home joyfully with the money. He decided to assuage his conscience by paying a tithe of ₦25 on it, not knowing that he was paying a demonic tithe. That is how many people pay demonic tithes after acquiring wealth with their satanic methods.

The list of satanic suggestions are endless. The devil generally tries to influence you to do what he knows is against the will of God. He will tell you: "Your finger nails are too short. Why don't you buy artificial finger nails, paint it in mermaid colours and stretch forth your hand and your fingers anywhere you go?" That is a very good satanic suggestion.

The devil has one strange pattern of behaviour. He generally reels into some kind of evil laughter as soon as he has succeeded in achieving his goal. Then he goes away leaving the person to struggle with the consequences of the violation of the word of God.

The power of satanic suggestion is so strong that it made Jesus to sweat blood.

Satan manipulates the mind of God's people by offering suggestions that look interesting and appealing to them.

THE MIND OF MAN AND DEMONIC MANIPULATIONS

Why are people finding it easier to accept satanic suggestions? Why are people finding it difficult to remember the Scriptures which they memorised? Why do the mind of people wander about during prayer? Why do people who are given wonderful revelations by God wake up in the morning only to forget all these revelations? These things take place because the minds of most people are subjected to demonic manipulations.

The human mind can be likened to a theatre where all forms of satanic operations take place. The extent to which you allow the devil to influence your thought is the extend to which he can control you. The devil will continue to control you as long as you continue to give him a free hand. You may say that you are speaking in tongues and that you are a spirit-filled Christian, all that will mean nothing to the devil as long as he continues to exercise dominion over your mind.

The human mind is the devil's greatest weapon. Without access to the human mind, the devil will not be able to do anything. The problems of most people originate from the human mind. All these show us that, the mind is the centre of serious warfare.

The devil has an instant and easy access to the mind of most people. Nothing is hidden from the devil. He has a complete picture of your mind, your thoughts, and your imaginations. Your motives, your intentions as well as your secret ambitions, are all known to him. He is thoroughly familiar with your weaknesses and strength. If you permit him to work on your mind he will go ahead to plant evil ideas there.

The devil knows us mo re than most of us know

ourselves. We often forget our past mistakes and overlook our weaknesses but the devil does not. The devil stores every information which he ever found in our hearts. He uses them to give us suggestions regarding what he wants us to do.

Once the devil knows that something is your weakness, he goes ahead to use it against you. If he knows that you are easily moved to tears, he will bring situations that will make you to cry. He knows that once you cry, you will be discouraged. He also knows that the moment you are discouraged you will not be able to pray. He will programme such situations into your life until you are completely prayerless. Then he will strike you with a very terrible attack.

You have to fight hard against all satanic suggestions. Once the devil tries a weapon against you and it works, he will continue to use that weapon against you until you are completely swept off your feet.

If your problem is fighting, or constant squabble, he will bring a lot of people who are ready to put up a fight against you.

If the devil knows that you are a worry bag he will constantly bring around you things that will make you to worry. But if you say no to all satanic suggestions, his weapons will become ineffective in your life. He will begin to try new areas.

The devil has continued to use the same method against human beings. He has continued to design evil suggestions in such a clever manner to make those suggestions match the weaknesses of people. He is not foolish, he does not give any suggestion that does not agree with your own feelings or desires. He generally gathers problems and places them on the platform of your background and peculiarity.

When these suggestions come they appear attractive as the best things to do. The devil uses his suggestions as weapons for achieving his goals. The devil will make you to cooperate with unbelievers, join your business with them and make them your confidants. The alliance will appear beautiful and effective on the out worthy. It will look like a good marriage. You may even go about rejoicing, thinking that you are surrounded by good people. While this is going on, powers of darkness will be having a good laugh at you.

A sister went to a man of God and said, "Please, pray for me, I want to get married." The man of God decided to do everything within his power to help the sister. He even went to a prayer mountain where he prayed for seven days to find out God's mind concerning the sister's marriage. He fasted non-stop for seven days. He then came down from the mountain with divine instructions for the sister. The man, God wanted the sister tomarry turned out to be blind in one eye. The sister found it difficult to accept a one-eyed man as God's will for her. She made up her mind that she was going to disobey God and look for a man to present to her friends and colleagues.

She actually succeeded and got married to a handsome man. Five years later, she lost her husband. The devil became happy, having succeeded in giving her an evil suggestion.

The devil is an expert in offering suggestions that appear good and beneficial. He gives suggestions which are aimed at leading men and women into deception. Once he succeeds in manipulating the mind, physical and mental ailments will follow.

It will also lead to failure, defeat, poverty, family breakdown, oppression, suicide, chronic sickness, profitless hard work and other forms of evil attacks. The devil will bring terrible problems and attacks into the lives of its victims because the minds have been captured.

Your life is determined by the state of your mind. The mind is the gateway to the spirit, soul and body. Your thought will determine your actions and your actions will determine your destiny.

Once again, I want you to close your eyés as you take this prayer point:

Oh Lord, shine Your divine light into my mind and let all strangers flee.

Did you take that prayer point with every spiritual energy within you?

Now you must lay your hand upon your chest as you take this aggressive prayer point:

Oh Lord, let Your kingdom be established in every department of my life.

CONSCIOUS AND SUB-CONSCIOUS MIND

Let me state this for the umpteenth time. Your life is determined by the state of your mind. Your mind is the sum-total of what is fed into it. Your mind is the gateway to your soul, spirit and body.

The mind of man consists of two departments. There is the conscious mind and the sub-conscious mind. The conscious mind is the smallest compartment in the human mind. On the other hand, the sub-conscious mind is what you make use of for what happens to you on the spot.

The sub-conscious mind is made up of memories that are long as well as a summary of all that has happened to you since you were born. Childhood experiences are stored in the mind. Traumatic experiences and other experiences that are embedded in the hearts of men are also stored up in the

brimful experience comes into contact with daily experiences that border on stubborn problems, the mind will become totally insane.

You accept forgiveness of sin in your conscious mind. Since the sub-conscious mind forms the greater part of the human mind, it has more impact upon our lives. Therefore, the sub-conscious mind must be renewed, changed, programmed and transformed by the word of God. The sub-conscious mind must conform to Christ if you want the totality of your heart to be wholesome. Failure to do this is to put your life under evil control.

Your mind must become the mind of Christ if you must experience total conformity to the character of Jesus Christ.

You must not give yourself any rest until the totality of what is stated in Philipians 4:8 becomes your experience.

Finally, brethren, whatsoever things are true, whatsoever things are honest, whatsoever things are just, whatsoever things are pure, whatsoever things are lovely, whatsoever things are of good report; if there be any virtue, and if there be any praise, think on these things.

Your mind could be pre-occupied with these thoughts. The moment you meditate upon anything outside these virtues you will bring your mind under evil control.

ATTACK AGAINST THE MIND

Your mind may be attacked in the following seven ways.

I   Attack by the forces of Egypt - What are the forces of Egypt? The forces of Egypt are the powers that fight against one's spiritual progress. When satan and his agents begin to fight against your spiritual progress or spiritual advancement, you are under the attack of the forces of Egypt.

The purpose of such attack is to revert you back to your old lifestyle, your former spiritual condition and your unregenerated nature. The spirit of worldliness will begin to attack you, telling you to go back into the world.

The spirit of Egypt will tell you, "You have been born again for ten years and no man has ever proposed marriage to you, why don't you go back to the world? Beautiful Ladies like you are always in high demand." If you agree with the suggestion, the devil will manufacture a thorough satanic man from the marine kingdom. He will give you a husband within a few months.

Once you agree with the devil, he will capture you. Your life and your calling will be swallowed up by evil powers. The greatest tragedy that can happen in the life of anyone who has been born again is for such a person to begin to use demonic charms. What will such a person say when he gets to heaven? Will he say that the devil is more powerful than God?

A friend of mine who happened to be a foreign minister of the gospel went somewhere to preach and had the most shocking experience of his life. He attracted the anger of an irate mob when he told them to give their lives to Jesus. They told him to stop mentioning the name of Jesus or face the option of being mobbed to death. He was told: "Leave us alone. We want to serve the devil." He was almost wounded. He decided to make further enquiries and later discovered that the majority of the crowd were born into the church.

It is very clear that anybody that was trained in the house of the Lord and turns his or her back at God, and goes to serve the devil, or to commercialise the gift of God, will find himself or herself in a serious trouble.

The function of the spirit of Egypt is to cause backward a movement. It, leads men and women to infantile behaviour.

I am aware of the fact that some members of our church are running from one group to another, looking for places of comfort. When such people make up their mind to join a particular group they are often told, "We have a lot of strict conditions in this group. We don't put on transparent dresses in this place. Such transparent dresses are as good as window blinds."

Such people will run to another group hoping to find a place that will accommodate their transparent dresses. They get to a new group and they are told, "Sorry madam, we can't admit you as a member of this group, your finger-nails are too long. They look like the claws of a demon. Why don't you cut them off?" Then the ladies may reply, "I cannot part with my finger nails. I have kept those nails for years." Then she runs away from that group to another group where she is told: "Sorry madam, we can't allow people like you to function in this group since we major on deliverance. We simply cannot allow you to put your serpentine chains on." That is how they go from one group to another.

Such people are affected by the spirit of Egypt. They eventually run away from the church. They spend their time going from one church to another until they discover that they are not able to find a place that thoroughly meets their spiritual needs. Some of them are already coming back to our church.

II Forces of repression - These forces specialise in repressing the lives of men and women. Repression is the opposite of expression. To express yourself means to be able to actualise all your goals.

The forces of repression work on the mind. Their

purpose is to repress the mind. They exact all kinds of forces on the mind holding it back from making any kind of progress. They will hinder you fr om growing up spiritually. These forces will allow you to be very busy leaving no time for spiritual matters.

III Forces of suppression - They suppress the spiritual lives of people with fear. Such people are always afraid even when there is no cause for alarm. They are always afraid of venturing to take authority over the powers of darkness.

A sister ran to the church because she had a serious problem. She discovered that, strange people were always killing fowls in front of her house on a daily basis. She once took a friend, to the front of her house when traces of blood were still visible. Her friend became fearful, as soon as she saw blood stains on the ground. But she decided not to disclose her fears. She simply told her friend that God has given her a revelation that a prayer should be said in the church. She persuaded her to come to the church to cancel the effects of the evil sacrifice. The sister accepted.

As they were going on the way, her friend suddenly complained of some health problems, asking to be excused from the prayer meeting. That was how she practically disappeared from the scene as a result of fear. She allowed forces of suppression to work upon her mind.

IV   Forces of depression - This spirit brings depression and heaviness into the minds of people. It makes people low-spirited, gloomy and despondent. Their primary goal is to sadden and discourage the minds of men and women.

V   Forces of oppression - Oppressive forces are forces that press people down. They lead to worry and anxiety. They make the mind to be bothered by all kinds of thing. They bring worry as well as physical and mental problems to the lives of people. Ninety per cent of church-goers experience one form of oppression or the other. Some of these operations lead to obsession.

These forces besiege the mind in an abnormal manner. They programme the mind into taking wrong decisions. Once a single wrong step is taken, powers of oppression take over completely.

VI Forces of obsession - These forces dominate the lives of people. They put men and women under complete control. They cause all kinds of problem the mind, leading their victims farther away from God. By the time their actions are completed their victims become mad.

When satan is allowed to have complete access into the lives of men or women he goes for the total control of their minds. He makes the mind to be totally out of the victim's control. He can take the mind to the highest level of madness. He will continue to do that until his victim is destroyed physically, spiritually and in every realm of life.

VII How about the 7th way by which the mind may be attacked?

WAY OUT

How then can we solve the problem of the madness of the mind? What steps must we take to take every form of malady away from the heart? What must you do if your heart has been invaded by the devil? What scriptural steps and principles must you follow to keep your heart away from evil domination?

- *Recognise that there is a problem.*

- *Accept the Lord Jesus Christ fully.*

- *Surrender totally to Christ.* One fact which you must bear in mind is that every unsurrendered aspect of your life gives room to the devil.

- *Commit yourself completely to the Lord Jesus.*

- *Commit yourself to studying the word of God.*

- *Pray evil trees out of your life.*

You must carry out all these steps if you want to have a wholesome mind. Demons know whether you have surrendered yourself to Christ.

A sister came for prayer because she noticed that several things were wrong in her family. She discovered that things began to go haywire as soon as she employed a housemaid. The housemaid was so effective, agile and hard-working that no other one could match her strength and ability.

The housemaid wakes up 4.00 in the morning and puts everything in the house in order. By the time the family gathered together for quiet time in the mornings he has already prepared breakfast. The husband and the wife were so impressed that they doubled her salary, thinking that they were fortunate to have such a hardworking person in their family.

However, the sister began to notice that everybody in the family began to complain of one ailment or the other The straw that broke the camel's back was the decision of the maid to attack the sister by using her spiritual power. She made a small mistake when the sister was traveling to England. The sister gave her a few strokes of the cane only to discover that her hand became swollen within a few minutes. The ban was so unbearable that the sister had to rush to my house. It took warfare prayers to deal with the problem. We also discovered that there was a problem in the life of the sister which gave the maid an opportunity to attack the members of her family. The sister suffered demonic attack because she had demonic problems in her mind. What happened to her should be a lesson for all careless Christians.

PRAYER POINTS

1. Every power of familiar spirits and every power of witchcraft working against my life, release me now, in the name of Jesus.

2. I frustrate every demonic arrest over my mind, in the name of Jesus.

3. Holy Ghost fire, destroy every satanic plantation in my mind, in the name of Jesus.

4. I bind every spirit withholding my testimony in life, in the name of Jesus

5. Every river of backwardness flowing into my mind, dry up, in the name of Jesus.

6. Everv evil association with unfriendly friends, break now, in the name of Jesus.

7. I destroy anything that is representing me in any demonic meeting, in the name of Jesus.

9

Spiritual Diagnosis of the mind

The Bible itemizes and describes the diseases of the mind, just as it also highlights the diseases of the tongue.

These mind diseases are generally suffered by men and women.

Let us enumerate and examine them.

Hearts that are full of iniquity - The Bible says:

The heart is deceitful above all things, and desperately wicked: who can know it? (Jer 17:9).

Unclean hearts - What makes people unclean is the heart, not the garment.

Perverse heart - The Bible says.

A froward heart shall depart from me: I will not know a wicked person (Ps 101:4).

The human heart is generally perverse. This explains why a lot of people keep malice for several years.

I sometimes feel sorry for marriage counselors. They often get embarrassed whenever they are trying to settle some quarrels. The wife might say "Man of God, kindly allow me to say one or two things. God bless you, sir. I wish you more anointing. Kindly allow me to consult my diary to prove my case. He did the same thing at exactly three O'clock on 5th March 1992. He also did the same thing in 1993, 1994 and 1995. It didn't stop there. He also did the same thing in 1997 and early 1999. I don't think he will ever stop offending me that way. I can never forget what he has done."

That is an evidence of the presence of being perverse in the heart. People who are perverse in the heart cannot walk with God as long as they continue to bear grudges in their heart.

Some people are so full of conceit, that they wont say a word to anybody until they have carried out the evil that is locked up in their hearts. Such people generally go ahead to incubate the evil in their hearts. When they carry out the evil, those who are around them will go ahead to express surprise. "Why should such a gentle person like you do this? You've always been so pleasant that we thought you wouldn't be able to hurt a fly."

Such people would say, "You haven't seen anything yet. Don't you ever take me for granted. I am a green snake under a green grass." Something is wrong with the heart.

Some people sing thus, "Holy Ghost fire, fire fall on me like the day of Pentecost, fire fall on me." As soon as the fire of God comes into the congregation it begins to examine the people one by one. When the Holy Ghost looks at the first worshipper, He says, "This person can't withstand My power. He is not qualified to receive the power he is asking for. His life is not right with God. If I fall on him he may collapse as a result of the conflict of powers." The Holy Ghost will go ahead to fall on only those who are ready within the congregation.

Is your heart perverse? If it is, it cannot receive the anointing of the Spirit of God.

Blind heart - The Bible says:

Because that, when they knew God, they glorified him not as God, neither were thankful; but became vain in their imaginations, and their foolish heart was darkened (Rom 1:21).

This passage shows that many people go about with blind or darkened hearts.

II Cor. 4:4 also says:

In whom the god of this world hath blinded the minds of them which believe not, lest the light of the glorious gospel of Christ, who is the image of God, should shine unto them.

This makes it very clear that the person who blinds the heart of men and women is the devil.

Mad heart - The hearts of some people is outrightly

mad. The Bible says:

> **This is an evil among all things that are done
> under the sun, that there is one event unto
> all: yea, also the heart of the sons of men is
> full of evil, and madness is in their heart
> while they live, and after that they go to the
> dead (Eccl 9:3).**

This passage explains why the heart of several men and women are never settled. The hearts of most people today are in shambles. The whole of the heart is in disarray. Such people go from one trouble to another. They are generally unreasonable and confused. Such hearts need deliverance, for they are not under the control of the Holy Spirit. It is being controlled by the devil.

The moment the gentle dove gets into such a troubled heart, there will be a great calm. Some people come to us saying, "I don't know why I hear voices in my ears." Such people are looking at the wrong thing. Such noises are first words in the hearts before they are heard through the ears.

Doubtful or unstable heart - Another important disease of the mind is doubt and unstability. The Bible says:

> **They speak vanity every-one with his
> neighbour: with flattering lips and with a**

double heart do they speak (Ps 12:2).

A doubtful heart is a double heart. It is neither here nor there. It is unstable. The eighth verse of the first chapter of the Epistle of James also tells us that

A double minded man is unstable in all his ways.

He is likened to the waves of the sea that are tossed here and there. The Bible states very clearly thatsuch a double minded man should not expect any answer to his prayers. A doubtful mind, therefore, is unstable, skeptical, unreliable and uncertain. Such a heart is not under the control of the Holy Spirit.

It is crystal clear therefore, that if something is not under the control of the Holy Spirit, it is under the control of the devil. What kind of heart do you have? Is your heart doubtful? Does it waver? Are you neither here nor there? If you allow doubt in your heart the devil will take control of your heart. You will become a victim of madness of the mind.

The heart can be hardened - A hardened heart is a heart controlled by the devil. The Bible says:

For they considered not the miracle of the loaves: for their heart was hardened (Mark 6:52).

Those who have this kind of heart are generally

stubborn. They turn deaf ears to the word of God. When God speak to them, they refuse to obey. They harden their hearts. No human being can continue to have opportunities for life.

The Bible says, **"Today is the day of salvation."** It also declares: **"Now is the acceptable time."** And it goes ahead to say: **"Today, if ye hear his voice harden not your hearts as it was in the day of provocation."**

Those who make up their minds that they are going to do what is in their hearts regardless of what God is saying to them are playing with destruction in time and in eternity.

Hardness of the heart is one of the most dreadful diseases that can plague the human heart. A man or a woman whose heart is hardened is an enemy of God. Hardness of the heart is one of the worst offences which anyone can commit against God. Incidentally, there is no room for hardness of heart for any believer in the New Testament.

This was made very clear when the disciples of the Lord Jesus came to Him. They wanted to know why divorce was permitted under the Old Testament dispensation. Jesus told them clearly that it was permitted by Moses because of the hardness of the heart of the people who lived in those days. This shows us that, in the New Testament, hardness of the heart is an aberration. It is not supposed to be mentioned among God's people.

God has made the possession of a tender heart possible through the sacrificial death of Jesus on the cross. Through His sanctifying grace, our hearts can be soft and full of the grace of God.

A lot of what goes on today in the name of religion runs contrary to the word of God. There is nothing like a 'stubborn believer'. A true child of God is not supposed to stick to his guns regardless of what God is saying. If your heart is hardened, something is wrong somewhere. If you go about saying, "This is my decision, I am holding to my principle, no human being can change me. I have made up my mind. That's just the way I am," such statements portray the fact that your heart is hardened. It is far away from the mind of Christ. The only person you resemble through that character is the devil.

If your heart is hardened, it is a clear indication that it is sick. And if you allow such a heart to keep on controlling you, it will surely lead you to hell.

Proud hearts - Pride is another major disease of the heart. It is such a terrible disease that will manifest openly no matter how hard you try to conceal it. All those who are proud give expression to their pride in one way or the other.

Pride will make you feel and act as if you are superior to other people. When it is treasured up in the heart, pride will make you to behave as if you are greater than everyone else. The Bible says:

> **Before destruction the heart of man is haughty, and before honour is humility (Prov 18:12).**

Those who are proud generally conduct themselves in haughty ways. They go about parading themselves as people who are greater or better than others.

Again the Bible says:

> **Whoso privily slandereth his neighbour, him will I cut off: him that hath an high look and a proud heart will not I suffer (Ps 101:5).**

One characteristic feature of all those who have pride in their hearts is that they go about trying to showcase themselves to everyone who comes across them. They place their achievements, graces, virtues, talents or possessions on the shelf where everyone can see them. They raise their shoulders higher than that of their neighbours and colleagues. They raise their voices louder than the voices of all the people around them. They highlight what they have done or achieved while they play down what others have done.

Those who are proud are easily identified in the society. When they dress, they make sure that their dresses make them to stand out from the crowd. They try to do everything to impress those who are around them.

Are you proud of anything? Do your achievements in life make you proud? Do you go about parading yourself as if you are better than all the other brothers and sisters? Do you draw attention to yourself?

The Bible says:

And seekest thou great things for thyself? seek them not: (Jer 45:5).

Pride will not do you any good. Rather it will make you a companion of the devil.

Pride starts from the heart. Then, it goes on to affect every department of your life. In the same vein, humility starts from the heart. If you come across a believer whose life is characterised by humility such a believer surely has a humble heart.

Those who are proud generally find it difficult to take lowly position in the church. If you create a Sunday school class whose members include university professors, engineers, lawyers, doctors, top business professionals and wealthy men and women, they will not accept any teacher who does not belong to their category to teach them. Such an attitude denotes pride.

Some people come to the church with their shoulders raised very high. They tell those who listen to them, "I can't just join any group in this church. I know my class and I'm looking for it. Do you expect me to seat down with carpenters, traders and all these common people in our society? Of course, not. I must look for my class and identify with it." You are proud if that describes your attitude. There is no class in the church. We are all equal before the Almighty.

Have you discovered that those who are proud are generally the poorest, spiritually speaking? One thing, which those who are class conscious must remember is the fact that, the greatest problem of their lives came into existence through association with people in their class. Why must such people come to the church looking for a class? This attitude is a symbol of pride.

Jesus Christ, we are told, was lowly. Are you lowly or are you proud? If you go about looking for your class you may find it in hell.

Hypocritical heart - Hypocrisy is another terrible disease of the heart. If your heart is filled with hypocrisy, you will behave like an hypocrite everywhere you go. The Bible says:

> **He answered and said unto them, Well hath Esaias prophesied of you hypocrites, as it is written, This people honoureth me with their lips, but their heart is far from me (Mark 7:6).**

Hypocrisy is one of the most terrible diseases that can plague the human heart. Those who are hypocrites often parade what they are not before others.

Those who are hypocrites generally go about parading fake smiles when their hearts are filled with hatred and anger. Some people go about destroying their neighbours. Those who do such things are actively working for the devil. That is why we have stated time and again that the devil's best work is done by God's people.

A lot of Christians go about spreading idle tales. They gossip, backbite and exaggerate little facts beyond measure. Whenever they find a listening ear they say, "Have you heard what brother so and so has done? Do not say I told you."

They go to another person who is idle like them saying "Have you heard about what happened to Pastor Paul? Don't let anyone know that I'm the one who revealed the secret. Keep whatever I'm going to tell you to yourself." This same people will go ahead to shake hands and crack jokes with the people whom they have just gossiped about. That is a mark of hypocrisy.

We have always made our stand known concerning that kind of ungodly behaviour. If someone comes to us saying, "I have come to discuss what brother A has just done." We normally tell such people: "Can you stop what you are saying right there? We are going to call brother A to come face to face with you and you are going to repeat what you have just said before him." If the gossip is unwilling to fa ce the person whom he or she is gossiping about, we normally take disciplinary measures against him. Gossips are Achans in conduct and believers in outward appearance. They are first class hypocrites.

God hates hypocrisy, with perfect hatred. He specifically states, "The hope of the hypocrites shall vanish."

Deciding to sit on the fence is a mark of hypocrisy. You must conduct your affair in such a way that all those who know you will know where you really stand. Steer clear of hypocrisy. If you must be a Christian, go deeper with the Lord. You must have nothing to do with half measures. Placing one leg on the mountain and the other one in the valley will take you nowhere. You must possess everything which God has earmarked for you. Those who stay at the middle point will end up collecting the arrows which are fired by serious Christians and those which are fired by demonic agents. They will receive double attacks because they are neither here nor there.

Covetous hearts - Covetousness is a major spiritual heart disease which majority of Christians suffer in this modern era. The Bible says:

Take heed, brethren, lest there be in any of you an evil heart of unbelief, in departing from the living God (Heb 3:12).

The passage you have just read points to the type of heart that is ungodly. The preceding verses have much to say concerning the covetousness of the children of Israel.

Peter, the apostle, talks of eyes full of adultery, and that cannot cease from sin; beguiling unstable souls: an heart they have exercised with covetous practices; cursed children (2 Peter 2:14). This passage reveals that covetousness leads to a curse. A covetous heart runs after everything, including what is unnecessary.

What kind of heart do you have? Is your heart filled with covetousness? Are you so covetous that you can eliminate other people to satisfy the covetous longings of your depraved heart?

Covetousness is a deadly spiritual disease. Those who fail to deal with covetousness will end up in hell fire.

Wicked heart - A wicked heart is malicious and ungodly. The presence of wickedness in the heart does not mean that one whose heart is wicked should only be compared with notorious men and women in the society.

Christians are always very quick to excuse themselves in this regard. Wickedness is not measured in terms of quantity. The presence of any iota of wickedness in your heart qualifies you as a wicked man or a wicked woman. It is unfortunate that most people whose hearts are occupied by wickedness are completely ignorant about it.

The Bible says:

The sacrifice of the wicked is abomination: how much more, when he bringeth it with a wicked mind? (Prov 21:27).

The Bible underscores the fact that the heart can be wicked. What kind of heart or mind do you have?

Foolish hearts - A foolish heart is generally stupid and unintelligent. The Bible says:

A fool uttereth all his mind: but a wise man keepeth it in till afterwards (Prov 29:11).

What kind of heart do you have? What is the state of your heart? Is your heart filled with the wisdom of God or foolishness? What kind of thoughts and ideas emanate from the fountain of your heart? Are they wise thoughts and ideas or are they foolish thoughts and ideas?

It is indeed shameful for a child of God to go about with hearts that are filled with foolishness. If your heart is characterised by foolishness you surely need a divine surgical operation on it.

Carnal hearts - The Bible says:

Because the carnal mind is enmity against God: for it is not subject to the law of God, neither indeed can be (Rom 8:7).

A carnal mind will always think about carnal things. Carnal hearts are generally filled with worldly materialistic and ungodly thoughts. The prayer points of a carnal mind are mostly centred on worldly things.

The preoccupations of the modern day Christians is centred on worldly things. This is a great departure from what the Bible teaches in Matthew 6:33:

But seek ye first the kingdom of God, and his righteousness; and all these things shall be added unto you (Matt 6:33).

Those who seek other things instead of seeking the kingdom of God are putting the cart before the horse. Such people are operating their lives contrary to the divine blueprint. A terrible curse hangs upon the head of all those who contradict the word of God.

If your heart is filled with carnality, it is a clear indication of the fact that you have chosen to run your life contrary to the Word of God. The psalmist declares:

I have been young, and now am old; yet have I not seen the righteous forsaken, nor his seed begging bread (Ps 37:25).

I challenge you to show me a truly righteous man who is poor.

Vain hearts - Vain hearts are hopeless and non-productive. The Bible says:

This I say therefore, and testify in the Lord, that ye henceforth walk not as other Gentiles walk, in the vanity of their mind, (Eph 4:17).

The ungodly generally walk in the vanity of their mind. They think vain thoughts and nurse vain values in their minds.

Corrupt mind - This is another kind of heart that needs deliverance. A corrupt heart is debased, erroneous and decayed.

The hearts of many so-called Christians are so full of corruption that should they open their mouths and let out the amount of corruption that is stored there, they will be odious to the ears of God and those of the righteous. If God were to rip open the hearts of many people, their contents will be embarrassing. If the thoughts of such hearts were to be relayed over the microphone, shame will cover the faces of their owners.

It is very easy for men and women whose hearts are filled with corruption to hide the contents of their hearts from those who are close to them. The Bible says:

> **. . . for the LORD seeth not as man seeth; for man looketh on the outward appearance, but the LORD looketh on the heart (1 Sam 16:7).**

Weary mind - Weariness of the mind is a deadly disease that must be dealt with. The Bible says:

> **For consider him that endured such contradiction of sinners against himself, lest ye be wearied and faint in your minds (Heb 12:3).**

This passage shows us that the heart could be tired or be under stress.

TYPES OF HEART IDENTIFIED BY JESUS

The descriptive analysis of the human mind which we have undertaken so far shows us that there are many mind con ditions that require deliverance and urgent rescue. It becomes clear therefore, that the mind can minister death or life. This explains why Jesus, in His teaching, divided the human hearts into seven categories. Here are the seven types of hearts which Jesus identified:

1. The heart can be hardened to spiritual realities.

2. The heart can be blind and incapable of seeing what is clear to a spiritual person. In other words, a heart that is blind will not be able to see things from the spiritual stand point.

3. Jesus told us that the heart, and not the brain is the point where sin begins.

4. Jesus told us that the words which we speak are first conceived in the heart before they are uttered through the mouth.

5. Jesus told us that the devil operates his powers on the heart of man.

6. Jesus told us that doubt begins in the heart.

7. Jesus also told us that sorrow and troubles parade

the corridors of the mind.

Therefore, when we talk about deliverance, it covers many areas of life. Stated explicitly, deliverance could be for the body, soul or spirit. When someone becomes born again, it is the spirit or the inner mind that experiences transformation. Your soul or your mind still needs to be renewed with the word of God.

Therefore, there are many powerful spirits that influence the heart, the spirit or the mind of people. Some of these forces or demons are so powerful that they sometimes bring out the real spirit of their victim and replace it with an evil spirit.

Some wicked spirits specialise in carrying out evil assignments against the heart of men and women. However, these assignments are no longer carried out on your spirit the moment you become born again. That is why the Bible commands us to renew our minds through the word of God, and to surrender our bodies unto the Lord, so that He will exercise total control over them leaving no room for the devil.

How then do we explain the cases of believers who love the Lord but experience nightmares and evil attacks in the realm of the dream? Why do children of God experience attacks in their dreams? Why are some people pursued by masquerades and agents of darkness in their dreams? Why are the lives of many Christians besieged by mind-controlling forces?

The answer is unmistakably clear. Your spirit got born again but your mind and your body must be totally surrendered unto God and kept away from anything that can stand as an enemy of God. You must also ensure that your heart is kept away or secured from all evil dominations.

If the mind is so important, it becomes clear that we need the deliverance of the mind if we must enjoy our walk with God and our lives here on earth. I am not contesting the fact that you are a child of God. It is possible to be born again and yet have your state of mind in such a condition that it is very far away from what God expects from you. It is also possible for you to claim that you are a child of God and go about with a mind that is under evil domination.

Are you tired about the condition of your mind? Are there certain things that go on in your mind, which you know, run contrary to your heart desires? Do you occasionally find engage yourself in thoughts that are foreign to the life of a true child of God? Have you tried without any success to control what goes on in your mind? Have you tried to shut up some thoughts from your mind only to find them coming back the next moment?

Have certain things crept into your mind which you would prefer that no human being must know about? Are you embarrassed by the quality and the nature of thoughts that occupy your heart on a daily basis?

If you cannot answer these questions sincerely then it is clear that you have a serious problem.

The nature of your problem is clear. There is a great gap between where your heart is right now and the place God wants it to be. In other words, there is a very wide gap between the ideal heart that God wants you to possess and the present state of affairs in your mind. You surely have a great w ork to do. The gap must be reduced. The space between what God wants you to be and what you are must be filled.

If you allow your mind to remain in a state where it is not in accordance with the word of God, you are leading a life that is risky.

You may be very popular in the church and you may be one of the busy Christians on earth, but if you have no time to look into your heart and to obtain wholesome healing and total deliverance of your heart, you are leading a wasted life.

The heart is the focus of God. God does not look at how you appear outwardly. He does not look at what you say or profess to be. His searchlight is always on state of things in your heart. If you fail to meet the divine condition concerning purity of heart, you have failed in everything.

A man who cannot control his heart cannot walk with

God. That is why the Bible says, "My son, give me thy heart." Again the Bible says, "Keep thy heart with all diligence, for out of it are the issues of life." If your heart falls short of the glory of God, you will not enter the kingdom of God. If you lose the battle of the mind, you have lost all the battle.

If your mind is placed side by side with the divine standard, how will your heart rate? If your heart misses the mark, you will surely miss heaven. All those who allow their minds to be turned into demonic market place, where all sorts of evil trafficking go on, will end up in hell fire.

Your personal opinion at this point, does not really matter. What matters is what God will say about your mind and your life at the end of your journey. You should not go about deceiving yourself today saying: "My mind is my property, I can nurse, think or entertain all kinds of thoughts that appeal to me, there is no problem." You can go ahead and allow your heart to be occupied by all kinds of thoughts that are ungodly. You may also allow your mind to be centred on evil affections. At the end, God will tell you, "Depart from me."

Remember the word of God "Man looketh on the outward appearance but God looketh on the heart." You can go to church in gorgeous dresses, you can shake everybody's hand, you can flash an infectious smile towards all those who come across you, but if your heart is dirty, ungodly and in an unhealthy condition, you are sure to receive divine judgement and "I never knew you" verdict at the end of your life.

Some have died and got to the gate of heaven thinking that they would be admitted with pageantry only to be disappointed. The angel of God told them, "Sorry, you can't come in here because there is anger in your heart." That was how they were denied entrance into heaven.

Thank God for the mercy of God. Some of them were allowed to come back to make amends. Some got to the gate of heaven only to be turned back and sent to hell fire. Such people often tried to put up a defence saying: "But I did not commit any sin. I did not kill anybody neither did I commit fornication." Such people were shocked when told, "Sorry we cannot allow you to come into heaven because you were always having evil thoughts concerning yourself."

Have you ever considered the fact that allowing evil thoughts to come into your hearts and settle down there can hinder you from getting to heaven? Do you know that doubt, discouragement and despair can get your heart into a state where it becomes unsuitable for the heavenly kingdom? Once you are disqualified from entering heaven, the only other available place is hell fire.

The issue of the mind is so serious that you must set a watch over it every moment of your life.

The judgement of the mind is so severe that no heart will be spared at the divine seat of judgement. The human heart is governed by imaginations and thoughts. Your life is controlled by the kind of thoughts entertain in your mind. Your conduct is the sum total of what you allow in your mind.

Some people sit down quietly and plan evil without anyone knowing about it. Others perfect evil and ungodly plans in the quietness of their hearts. The sins that men and women commit are first planned and determined in the heart before they are brought to the open in the form of evil and ungodly steps.

I want you to be sincere with yourself at this point. Think about certain bad things you did recently or a long time ago. Have you discovered that they were done because they were first entertained or meditated upon in the heart? Did you tell a lie? Did you allow lust in your heart or did you steal? None of these things would have happened to you suddenly without your allowing the thoughts in your heart.

Those who commit fornication or adultery generally spend a lot of time meditating upon such things before they happen in real life. People often wondered why some respected Christians fall into sin. Such people have not considered the fact that somebody can pray fire prayer without watching over his or her mind. Immediately the thoughts of your heart differ from the thoughts of Christ, satan and his demons will move their factory into your heart.

THE RIGHT MIND

If your mind is not in any of the following states, then you need deliverance of the mind.

Perfect peace - The world is in a disarray today because there is a lot of war going on in the mind of men and women. No war has ever taken place in any part of the world without being preceded by turmoil and war in the minds of the people. There will be no war on earth if peace can prevail upon the heart of every living man and woman.

Therefore, the wars that are going on in many parts of the world today are offshoots of the war that was going on in the minds of the average man. No one can declare a war without the heart of that man being in turmoil and confusion.

War is therefore transferred to aggression. The chaos come into the open and war is declared and people begin to waste their lives in battles that are simply unnecessary. If men take care of their hearts, no nations will ever need to go to war.

Let me bring this thought into the local community. Most of the crimes, evils and atrocities perpetrated in any community are always offshoots of the states of the mind of the perpetrators who are residents of that community.

Again, if we bring this thought into the family unit we will discover that there is war, squabble and misunderstanding because the heart of the father, the mother and the children are first embattled internally before that results in an open quarrel.

Somebody suddenly gets angry and begins to fight because the mind knew no peace. If your mind is peaceful, you will not fight anyone, nor will you speak angry or quarrelsome words.

Why do armed robbers break into people's houses? Why do they fire guns at innocent victims? The answer is very simple. The gunshots first went on in their minds before they are fired physically.

No crime is committed, no robbery is carried out and no evil is done without it emanating from the heart that lacks the peace of God.

I once heard the story of a university professor who was jailed because he was caught stealing bags of rice. He made a funny remark when the judge was passing the sentence on him. "Why must you send me to jail? Why don't you consider the feelings of the members of my village? I have been a great asset to them. Please, don't send me to jail because of my community." I wonder if he ever thought about the implication of his action on his community before he decided to steal a bag of rice.

The Bible says:

Thou wilt keep him in perfect peace, whose mind is stayed on thee: because he trusteth in thee (Isa 26:3).

Therefore, a healthy mind has a perfect peace. Your mind cannot be said to be healthy if there is the absence of perfect peace in it.

Humble mind - Paul, the apostle declared that he served God with humbleness of mind. A healthy mind is a humble mind.

Hearts that are transformed through renewal - The Bible says:

I beseech you therefore, brethren, by the mercies of God, that ye present your bodies a living sacrifice, holy, acceptable unto God, which is your reasonable service (Rom 12:1).

You need a transformed heart if you want your mind to be wholesome.

The mind of Christ - You would be said to be wholesome when you have the mind of Christ. Phil 2:5 says:

Let this mind be in you, which was also in Christ Jesus (Phil 2:5).

Do you have the mind of Christ?

A sound mind - This kind of mind is made very plain in II Tim 1:7 which says,

For God hath not given us the spirit of fear; but of power, and of love, and of a sound mind (2 Tim 1:7).

A sound mind is completely devoid of confusion. Those who have sound minds know how to give unto Caesar what is Caesar's and unto God what is God's. They know how to be firm when the issue of compromise is concerned. Such people will not supply alcohol during weddings. They would give their in-laws Nico sweet instead of alligator pepper.

Minds that are filled with wisdom - A healthy mind is generally filled with wisdom. You must ensure that your mind is filled with these virtues. You must get evil off your mind and bring grace into it.

Note what's on your mind. Do you have the spirits of confusion, fear, pride, criticism, poverty, violence, worry, envy, laziness, ignorance, depression, dejection, rebellion, exhibitionism, sexual perversion, deception, wicked imagination, frustration, greed, impatience, suicide, lack of concentration or uncontrollable thoughts? You must not allow any of these to dominate your mind.

You need to do an aggressive warfare prayer against all these. Here is the unmistakable declaration of the

Scriptures:

(For the weapons of our warfare are not carnal, but mighty through God to the pulling down of strong holds;) Casting down imaginations, and every high thing that exalteth itself against the knowledge of God, and bringing into captivity every thought to the obedience of Christ; (2 Cor 10:4-5).

HOW TO DELIVER THE MIND

How then can you deliver your mind?

1. Believe what God has said about the enemies of the mind.

2. Learn how these enemies operate.

3. Have a definite plan for resisting the enemy.

4. Know how to use your resources for Christ.

5. Incubate your mind with the Word of God. You must be a Bible addict.

6. Put up violent aggression against the enemy.

PRAYER POINTS

1. I rebuke all the spirits operating against the soundness of my mind, in the name of Jesus

2. I possess the mind of Christ, in the name of Jesus.

10

Deliverance of the mind

I want you to close your eyes and take this prayer point as a prelude to this chapter.

Let any strongman; delegated to monitor my life , be paralysed, in the name of Jesus.

A lot of people have continued to fight fake fires while leaving the real issues unattended to. Such people always complain saying, "I wonder why nothing seems to be working for me. I wonder why I have not achieved any tangible thing in spite of the fact that I have tried many methods to solve my problems."

Such people are yet to consider the fact that it is possible to spend the whole of one's life time applying the wrong method to a particular situation. No matter how hard you try, you will not achieve anything as long as you continue to use the wrong method.

Using a wrong method can be likened to a man who is going to move towards the direction of the west but begins to move towards the east. No doubt, such a person will make a lot of physical movements but he will find himself at the wrong end of the journey. Efforts made, money expended, time spent and energy used will all end up being wasted or squandered. If you focus on the wrong target you will end up being worse than a failure in life.

It is quite unfortunate that most people are spending their energy on none essentials instead of focusing on life's priorities. They are concentrating all the physical and the spiritual energy with which God has endowed them on things that are of no consequence in the light of eternity. One who takes such actions can be likened to a footballer who decides to play his own game outside the football pitch. No matter how skillful or active ·he is, nobody will reason with him. The relevance a of footballer is only in the field of play.

God wants us to concentrate our attention on the true condition of our hearts, but many children of God, are busy concentrating on what human beings can see and appreciate. If you go ahead and pre-occupy yourself with trivial matters, you will end up receiving condemnation from God.

Many believers are in trouble today because of their lack of giving proper attention to the mind. The more you take care of the state of your heart, the more wholesome your life will be.

If you open the door of your house and allow mosquitoes to fill the place only to go ahead to buy an insecticide, which you apply on the place without closing the door, you will discover, sooner or later, that you have not solved any problem. The mosquitoes will not be bothered as they will only give you some time before they return. They will stage a come-back, immediately the condition of the room becomes conducive for them. The only permanent solution to the problem is to either keep .the doors of your house closed, or fix nets on the windows and doors.

That is exactly what you must do to keep your mind free from corruption and evil contamination.

The Bible says:

Let the words of my mouth, and the meditation of my heart, be acceptable in thy sight, O LORD, my strength, and my redeemer (Ps 19:14).

A lot of truths are locked up within this Scripture which you have just read. The most prominent truth in it is this: the meditation of a person's heart may be either acceptable or unacceptable to God. This makes us to understand the fact that there are acceptable and unacceptable meditations.

The meditations of your heart are acceptable unto God when they conform with divine expectation. It is unacceptable when it is contrary to the word of God. Being a sharp shooter and a prayer addict, the psalmist, who wrote these words under the inspiration of the Holy Spirit, knew the importance of the frame of the mind in relation to receiving answer to prayers.

If you fail to take care of the disposition of your heart you will end up being disgraced publicly.

A brother once thought evil, only to be exposed by God. He was a Sunday school teacher and very effective in church activities. Members of the Sunday school class as well as other members of the church thought that he was one of the best Christians around. He was well favored by his pastor. The pastor's wife also viewed him as a very fine Christian. In fact, she formed the habit of giving the brother monetary and other gifts. She used to buy him shirts whenever she traveled to England. In one word, the brother was highly favored by every member of the church.

Nobody knew that he was battling with a serious defilement of the heart as well as unimaginable secret sins. The cat was let out of the bag when, one day, his pastor ran into him when he was busy smoking a stick of cigarette. The pastor was riding his sports bicycle, hence he was able to sight him from afar. As soon as the brother caught sight of his pastor he threw the stick of cigarette into his pocket thinking that his pastor would just greet him casually and leave.

The pastor brought his bicycle to a halt, came down and engaged him in a very long discussion. The fire of the cigarette kept on burning in the brother's pocket, yet he couldn't do anything about it.

The pastor noticed that the brother was feeling some discomfort as he kept on scratching his thigh. The cigarette continued to hurt his flesh. When the burns was becoming unbearable he began to dance. He continued to suffer in silence. The pastor kept on talking as if nothing was happening to the brother. The cigarette burnt its way out of his pocket and dropped on the ground. The brother looked at it and opened his mouth in bewilderment. The pastor saw it and went away sorrowfully. That was how what the young man tried to conceal was blown into the open.

A little boy came across a creature that looked like a small dog in a bush behind their house. He became fascinated, thinking that the animal was a special brand of the Alsatian dog. The animal looked so small, innocent and harmless. The young boy took the dog and hid it in the attic without telling his parents. Whenever he was given food he would share it into two equal halves and take the other half into the attic. He kept on feeding his pet without the knowledge of his parents.

When the parents noticed that the boy was fond of climbing into the attic they asked him what he always went up to do there. He did not know that he was nursing a young lion. His parents did not know that he was raising a young lion within their house. The young boy kept the secret to himself until he forgot to feed the lion for one whole week and a great tragedy befell the household. Before this time, the lion had become so accustomed to the boy that the boy did not sense any danger.

Whenever the boy was feeding the lion both of them generally played together. However, a hungry lion is no one's friend. The young boy suddenly remembered, after a busy week, that he had neglected his pet. He quickly carried some food and climbed the attic. He thought that the pet would play with him as usual. However, he discovered that the lion was somewhat weak. Before he could place the food on the floor the lion sprang up and descended on him. That was how he became the lion's meal that day. The young lion had its first human meal by converting his owner into food. The boy yelled and moaned until nothing was heard of him again. His parents rushed to the attic only to discover that they could only find parts and pieces of the body of their son.

The boy could have been rescued if he had not locked himself up in the attic. It was customary for the boy to lock himself up each time he was feeding the pet. This is another example of someone who has a dangerous property.

Others have invited destruction into their lives by handing out letters of invitation to the devil.

CATEGORIES OF DELIVERANCE CANDIDATE

Those who come for deliverance are generally divided into three categories.

1. Those who invite the enemies into their lives by inheritance.

2. Those who invite the enemy into their lives by personal decision.

3. Those who unconsciously, invite the enemy into their lives.

The third category is the most difficult group to deal with. Many people, these days, are busy consciously sending an invitation to the enemy. The most dangerous activity you can get involved in is to invite the enemy into your own mind. The danger becomes heightened when you are not aware of the problem.

If it is not free from evil influence, the mind will eventually land you into trouble. Your spiritual stamina notwithstanding, if you harbor a dangerous material in your mind you will crash in a terrible manner. You can make all kinds of claims about your spiritual stamina but if your mind has dirty properties in it you will not be able to stand upright. You will not know what it means to achieve success in every department of your life. In fact, you will continually remain a candidate for deliverance.

When you win a man's mind you have captured him. When you capture the thoughts of a person the person will come under your control. That is why satan fights tooth and nail, for the control of minds of men and women. The Bible says,

But I fear, lest by any means, as the serpent beguiled Eve through his subtilty, so your minds should be corrupted from the simplicity that is in Christ (2 Cor 11:3).

Satan corrupts, influences and manipulates the mind of people, including Christians. It is amazing that satan achieves his goals with amazing ease. For example, why are many Christians finding it difficult to memorise the Scriptures? The answer is simple: The devil is busy removing the word of God from their hearts.

Why do people's minds wander at the time of prayer? There is an evil force working on their minds. Therefore, the mind of man can be described as the theater of satanic operation.

The extent to which the devil influences your thought is the extent to which he can control you. The moment human beings no longer hand over their minds to the devil, he will be thrown out of business. The devil has nothing else to work with except human minds. Most of what he does in the lives of people generally start from their minds.

Therefore, the mind is the center of warfare. Most bodily afflictions operate from the mind. If you lose the battle in the realm of the mind you will lose the whole battle. If you win the battle in the realm of the mind then you have won the battle.

Satan has instant and immediate access to the mind of all men and women. It becomes your responsibility, therefore, to decide to barricade your mind against all kinds of satanic interference. The devil has a complete picture of all our thoughts and imaginations. He also has an access to all our motives whether those motives are pure or not.

Your innermost thoughts, your ambitions and all the thoughts which you feel no one knows about are known to the devil. In other words, nothing is hidden from the devil. He is also familiar with our weaknesses and our strengths. He knows your strong points, your defenseless areas as well as areas in which you are vulnerable.

He knows how to attack you and succeed. If you permit him, whether by carelessness or ignorance, he will go ahead to remove good ideas from your mind. He makes people to remember bad things and to forget good things.

He has a superb knowledge concerning what goes on on earth. It is surprising but true that he knows us more than we know ourselves. He stores all your faults and mistakes in his evil memory bank. He knows how to pick up what he has stored against you at the right time.

The devil is effective and masterly in the manner with which he works on human hearts. He offers suggestions that suit your weaknesses and shortcomings. He will also make sure that you forget what will make you think about pleasing God. That is why the Bible says: "There is a way

226

that seemeth right unto man but the end thereof are the ways of death."

A sister once came to see me with a funny prayer request. She said: "Man of God, just pray for me. I want to marry a pilot. I don't want to marry any other person except a pilot." I said to her: "Why don't you allow the Lord to choose for you? Don't choose a husband based on his profession." But she was so obsessed with her desire for a pilot that the devil manipulated her into getting outside the will of God. The devil succeeded in providing a pilot for her. The pilot showed his true colour by beating her up during the period of courtship.

She went ahead to get married to the pilot in spite of the fact that she had started turning her into a punching bag, even when they were not yet married. The devil got her into that condition by taking control of her heart.

The devil generally designs evil and clever suggestions matching them with our weakest points. He will go ahead to convince you that what he is telling you to do is for your welfare.

He is an expert in the art of deception and fabricating counterfeits. He is so experienced that you cannot play his evil game and win. You must be sincere with yourself.

Who is really in control of your mind? Can you truly say that the Holy Spirit has fully taken charge of your heart? If your mind is influenced and controlled by the spirit of

God, how then would you explain the presence of evil materials in your hand?

The devil's power of suggestion is so terrible that even the Lord Jesus was made to sweat in the garden of Gethsemane. The devil made Him to reconsider His stand concerning the cup of suffering. That was why Jesus prayed: "Father, make this cup to pass over Me." Thank God, He made up His mind to drink from the cup. He said, "Not My will but Thy will be done."

The greatest battle ground is the mind. Most battle grounds generally have two forces. The mind differs significantly in this direction. There are three forces fighting there: God, the devil and the flesh. The combination of these forces fight serious battles in the mind of man.

Most of the evil which people do are borne out of the influence of the human mind. People are influenced to do evil when their minds cooperate with the devil. That is why the psalmist prayed "Let the meditation of my heart be acceptable unto thee O Lord." What you are saying may sound good but your life will become unacceptable to God if the condition of your mind is unacceptable.

Nobody can deceive God. Man looks at the outward appearance while God looks at the heart. Your outward appearance may be captivating and dazzling but God will have nothing to do with you if your mind is in a state that is highly objectionable to him. It is possible to try to impress the pastor with your three piece suit or your expensive native dress, but God cannot be impressed by any of those things. If God were to be impressed by outward appearances, He would not have spoken to a man like Elijah. For example, Elijah did not wash his clothes for three years yet God spoke to him.

Evil and ungodly thoughts can be likened to opening the door of your heart for satanic garbage to be thrown into. Until your heart is brought under divine control you cannot experience a wholesome mind.

You must get to a stage in your life when your heart is lifted up to a height where it is totally in conformity with the mind of Christ.

You must not rest until you get to a point when it becomes natural for you to think godly thoughts. You have won a great battle if you can get to that level. It becomes easy, at that point, for you to receive your miracles and breakthroughs.

However, if you are still at the level where the enemy occupies your min1 completely and feed you with the bread of sorrow, you are a non-starter in the realm of spiritual growth.

If the devil can keep you depressed for the whole day, then he is the one controlling your life. You will not know what it means to exercise victory and dominion over the devil. Most of the people who come to church today are living on the fringe of divine blessings. Most of what they receive can be classified as an overflow of the blessings of God. They do not receive the real thing. They do not know what it means to receive the real showers of blessings; all they have are trickles. Such people often deceive themselves. They do not know that they cannot receive full blessings from God without possessing a wholesome mind. You cannot receive the blessings of God until you have experienced total deliverance of your mind.

The deliverance of your mind will usher great changes into your life. There are many wonderful experiences which you will never know until you allow God to renew your mind. The moment your mind receives a touch of transformation from the Almighty, you will begin to experience superlative blessings. Your experience will then agree with the words of the Scriptures: "He gave me beauty for ashes and the oil of joy for mourning and the garment of praise for the spirit of heaviness that he may be glorified."

To understand the meaning of receiving beauty for ash, you need to understand what ashes are used for. It was customary in those days for those who were bereaved or sorrowful to sprinkle ashes upon themselves. If you come across someone with ashes upon his or her head you will know, immediately, that he was either sorrowful or bereaved.

Those whose minds are free from evil domination generally experience the putting off of the garment of sorrow and the putting on of the garment of praise. Paul and Silas were surrounded by sorrow and they had every reason to resign to it. Nobody expected them to rejoice. What happened to them? They heard the voice of God telling them to go to Macedonia. They obeyed.

Something happened when they got to Philippi. They had an encounter with a very wealthy woman who was a seller of purple clothes. Purple clothes were used by extremely wealthy people in those days.

The wealthy woman got converted and decided to invite the men of God into her home. They were treated to an executive reception. It was a major breakthrough. However, there was a turn of events the next day, when Paul and Silas cast out a demon from a young girl. That was how they were attacked and dragged to the market place.

At last, they found themselves in the prison. By the time they were locked up in the prison, there were multiple wounds and bruises on their bodies. I am sure, you can imagine what it means to be dragged on the floor for a long time.

Whoever has gone through that experience would never forget the excruciating pain that went with it. Parts of the body would have been peeled off.

In those days, criminals were beaten with both cane and sharp objects. The person who went through that kind of experience would end up having his flesh seriously mutilated.

The physical environment in which they found themselves left them no room for anything but sorrow and sadness. The place was so dark that it was natural for it to induce gloom and despair in them.

Many people who find themselves in a pleasant environment often become moody and despondent. I wonder what such people would do if they should find themselves in harsh and hostile environment. What Paul and Silas went through was enough to make them complain bitterly. But there was no negative feeling in their minds which could have brought a negative response. Although their bodies were hurting, their minds were controlled by the Holy Spirit.

An average modern Christian would have broken down in tears. Others would go into ominous silence. They would have gone into the lower level of depression were they to be today's believers.

The first thing which we noticed about Paul and Silas is that they were able to pray. A lot of modern day believers are generally not able to pray whenever they have a little problem. Paul and Silas did not only pray, they also sang praises to God. The totality of their action and reaction showed that they were able to exercise control over what was going on around them.

If you allow what is going on around you to dictate the condition of your heart, you will welcome depression and discouragement. If you allow depression to feel your mind, you will miss the miracle that you are supposed to receive.

For Paul and Silas to have sung praises to God at midnight, they must have been in a high spirits. The midnight hour is the darkest hour for most people. Paul and Silas prayed and sang praises to the Lord until the prisoners heard them. A lot of Christians are not able to praise God whenever there is any negative condition around them, not to talk of raising up their voices to attract the attention of those who are around them.

Depression has made a lot of people to lose great blessings in life. If you allow the enemy to capture your mind and you become depressed you will lose great victories. One minute of depression may take 20 years miracle away from your life. The foundation of the prison would not have shaken and the doors would not have opened. The prisoners would not have been set free and the jailor would not have been saved if Paul and Silas had resorted to weeping or crying.

Are you putting on the garment of praise or are you overwhelmed by the spirit of heaviness? What is your response to the suggestions which the devil tries to bring into your mind? What is your reaction to the general economic situation in your country? Is your heart filled with faith or are you eating the bread of sorrow?

Are you dancing to the devil's tune? Are you playing the role which the devil wants you to play? Are you playing into the hands of the devil through what you allowed into your mind? Are you behaving as if all the problems in the world belong to you?

The Bible says, "For as he thinketh in his heart so is he." Your thoughts denote the kind of person you are. The troubles of most people begin in the mind. The heart or the mind is always God's starting point whenever He wants to work in your life. If God were to open the heart of everyone who comes into the church, a lot of people will become so embarrassed that they will never come to the church again.

The issue of the heart is so serious that the Scriptures reveal that the first time God destroyed mankind it was on account of the wrong state of the heart. "And God saw that the wickedness of man was great in the earth and that every imagination of the thoughts of his heart was only evil continually" (Gen. 6:5).

God sent judgement to man because He knew that all the evil things which were done were incubated in the heart.

Another instance of divine judgement in the Scriptures can be found in the 11th chapter of the book of Genesis.

And the LORD said, Behold, the people is one, and they have all one language; and this they begin to do: and now nothing will be restrained from them, which they have imagined to do. Go to, let us go down, and there confound their language, that they may not understand one another's speech. So the LORD scattered them abroad from thence upon the face of all the earth: and they left off to build the city. Therefore is the name of it called Babel; because the LORD did there confound the language of all the earth: and from thence did the LORD scatter them abroad upon the face of all the earth (Gen. 11:6-9).

God scattered the people because of the imagination of their hearts.

You must examine your heart today. What kind of thoughts do you entertain? Do you entertain evil thoughts in your heart while you go about speaking in tongues. The importance of taking care of the mind is stated in Prov. 4:23: "Keep thy heart with all diligence for out of it are the issues of life."

If you want to avoid being trapped by your tongue, you must watch what comes out of your mind, since what is spoken by the lips is determined by the state of the heart. You must s tart working on your mind to be wholesome in the realm of speech.

Conscious efforts must be made and serious warfare prayer must be carried out if you want to live a life completely free from bondage. If you will allow God to thoroughly work on your mind you will begin to speak the right words at all times. If you take care of everything else without taking care of the state of your heart you will continue to live in bondage. The moment your mind receives healing and deliverance you will experience a turn around in every area of your life.

PRAYER POINTS

1. Father, in the name of Jesus, I invite the ministry of deliverance into my mind.

2. You powers of darkness, release your hold upon my mind, in the name of Jesus.

3. I rebuke all the spirits operating against the soundness of my mind, in the name of Jesus.

4. I release my mind from bondage, in the name of Jesus.

11

This is war

PRAYER POINTS FOR THE FREEDOM OF THE MIND *Lord, strengthen me today to overcome my enemy.*

A. POWER AGAINST THE SPIRIT OF CONFUSION

1. I pull down, the strongh,old of the spirit of confusion in my life, in the name of Jesus.

2. Every city of confusion, within my mind, be broken down now, in the name of Jesus.

3. Let the storm of confusion within my mind be still, in the name of Jesus.

4. Every cloud, that has enveloped my mind, fade away now, in the name of Jesus.

5. I reject any form of confusion, I claim a sound mind, in the name of Jesus.

B. POWER AGAINST THE SPIRIT OF MIND DESTRUCTION

1. Any power that wants to destroy my life, I command

you to be destroyed, in the name of Jesus.

2. Every faulty foundation in my life, I command you to receive the fire of God, in the name of Jesus.

3. I shoot out, every evil arrow of mind destruction, fired against my life, to the sender, in the name of Jesus.

4. My mind, receive the touch of God and be renewed, in the name of Jesus.

5. Lord, strengthen me within my inner mind with Your fire and power.

C. DELIVERANCE FROM UNCONTROLLABLE THOUGHTS

1. I pull down, e very stronghold of uncontrollable thoughts in my life, in the name of Jesus.

2. I cast down, every evil imagination in my heart, in the mighty name of Jesus.

3. I bring into captivity, every area of my thought life to the obedience of Jesus Christ, in the name of Jesus.

4. In the name of Jesus, I break the power of evil remote controllers over my thought process.

5. I flood every doorway of evil uncontrollable thought

with the blood of Jesus.

D. CASTING DOWN IMAGINATIONS

1. I scatter into pieces, every evil imagination against me, in the name of Jesus.

2. I command all imaginations, contrary to my prayer life, to be defeated, in the name of Jesus.

3. I cast out and bring to nought, every demonic imagination against my family, in the name of Jesus.

4. I immunize my spirit, soul and body against every vain imagination, in the name of Jesus.

5. I cast down, plunder, and frustrate, every satanic imagination against my life, in the name of Jesus.

E. PULLING DOWN STRONGHOLDS OF IMAGINATION

1. Lord, I pull down, every stronghold of the enemy over my life.

2. I pull down and roast every demonic ladder, the enemy uses to enter my life, in the name of Jesus.

3. I come against evil pronouncements against my life, in the name of Jesus.

---

4. I arrest and bind every satanic notebook opening for my life, in the name of Jesus.

5. I cancel and nullify every evil imagination of the enemy upon my life, in the name of Jesus.

6. Blood of Jesus, cleanse my heart of every evil thought.

7. My heart, be delivered from every evil thought, in the name of Jesus.

8. I flee my heart, by the fire of the Holy Ghost, from every evil thought, in the name of Jesus.

9. Heavenly thought, fill my heart now, in the name of Jesus.

F. AUTHORITY AGAINST MIND CONTROLLING SPIRIT

1. You, my mind, in the name of Jesus, you will not push me to hell.

2. You habitation of darkness inside my mind, be desolate, in the name of Jesus.

3. Every evil attack on my mind, be defeated, in the name of Jesus.

4. You, my mind, receive the touch of fire, in the name of Jesus.

5. In the name of Jesus, I will make it in life.

6. Sting of death, release my mind, in the name of Jesus.

7. Sting of fear and failure, release my mind, in the name of Jesus.

8. I command all heavy burden in my life, to roll away and burn to ashes, in the name of Jesus.

9. Blood of Jesus, replenish my heart.

G. PARALYSING THE STRONGMAN WORKING AGAINST THE MIND

1. You power corrupting my desire and my mind, be roasted, in the name of Jesus.

2. You strongman of evil imagination paralysing good things in my life, be paralysed, in the name of Jesus.

3. Lord, revive my mind with Your fire.

4. Lord, put Your law into my mind.

5. All the good things that the strongman of the mind has paralysed, receive life and be restored to my life, in the name of Jesus.

H. LOCATING HIDDEN TREES IN THE MIND

1. I locate every hidden evil tree in my mind, with the fire of God, in the name of Jesus.

2. I uproot every evil hidden tree, in my mind. in the name of Jesus.

3. You, evil fruit, die, in the name of Jesus.

4. You, planters of evil trees in my life, be roasted, in the name of Jesus.

5. O Lord, begin to plant good things into my life and let them manifest in my life.

I. POWER AGAINST EVERY SPIRIT OF UNCERTAINTY

1. I bind and cast out, the spirit of uncertainty in my mind and I destabilise its control over my life, in the name of Jesus.

2. Holy Ghost, occupy every area that the spirit of uncertainty has in my mind, in the name of Jesus.

3. Father Lord, every damage that the spirit of uncertainty has done to my life, repair and restore it, in the name of Jesus.

4. I cast out every spirit of uncertainty in every area of my life, in the mighty name of Jesus.

5. I recover and possess every good thing that I lost to the spirit of uncertainty, in the name of Jesus.

J. SPIRIT OF MIND BLINDNESS

1. Holy Spirit, possess my mind, in the name of Jesus.

2. You spirit of mind blindness, loose your hold over my life, in the name of Jesus.

3. I renounce you spirit of mind blindness in my life, in the name of Jesus.

4. I regain my words, I regain my values, I regain my spiritual gift that I lost to the devil through the spirit of mind blindness, in the name of Jesus.

K. SPIRIT OF DEATH AND HELL

1. Throughout the days of my life, the gate of hell will not prevail over me, in the name of Jesus.

2. You, power of hell, release all my belongings that are under your control, in the name of Jesus.

3. As for me and my household, our name shall not enter the book of hell, in the name of Jesus.

4. You, spirit of death, you will not prosper in my life, in the name of Jesus.

5. I release the life of Christ into my life ,in the name of Jesus.

L. SPIRIT OF MIND WASTAGE

1. My mind, I command you to think aright, in the name of Jesus.

2. All mind controlling spirits, be bound, in the name of Jesus.

3. You, producer of evil thoughts, somersault and die, in the name of Jesus.

4. Holy Spirit, renew my mind to glorify God, in the name of Jesus.

5. Father Lord, soak my mind with heavenly revelations, in the name of Jesus.

M. DELIVERANCE FROM FRAGMENTED MIND

1. I gather together, every area of my mind, that is scattered, in the name of Jesus.

2. Every area of my life and mind in a satanic cage, be released, in the name of Jesus.

3. I plead the blood of Jesus into my mind and the whole of my life, in the name of Jesus.

4. I fire back, every arrow of the enemy fired into my mind, in the name of Jesus.

5. I command you, my mind, go back to your resting place, in the name of Jesus.

The 'TONGUE' TRAP

The tongue can be very destructive and unless you learn how to control it, that little organ of your body can set your life on fire. You are no longer a master of words once the words are spoken out.

The tongue has caused us more trouble than any other organ in the body. What has taken years to guild can be destroyed by the tongue in a few seconds. There are demons operating on the tongue.

This powerful book will teach you amazing secrets that would release tongues that are under bondage and propel tongues unto prosperity and life.

Read this book and your life will no longer remain the same.

About BCCM, MFM Ministries and the Author

Dr. Daniel Kolawole Olukoya, is the General Overseer of the Battle Cry Christian Ministries, and Mountain of Fire and Miracles Ministries (MFM). The Mountain of Fire and Miracles Ministries' Headquarters in Lagos, Nigeria is the largest single Christian congregation in Africa with an attendance of over 120,000 in any single meeting.

MFM, is a full gospel ministry, devoted to the revival of Apostolic signs, Holy Ghost fireworks, miracles and the unlimited demonstration of the power of God, to deliver to the uttermost. Absolute holiness within and without, as the greatest spiritual insecticide, and a pre-requisite for heaven, is openly taught. MFM is a do-it yourself gospel ministry, where your hands, are trained to wage war, and your fingers to do battle.

Dr. Olukoya, holds a first class honours degree in Microbiology, from the University of Lagos, Nigeria and a PhD in Molecular Genetics from the University of Reading, United Kingdom. As a researcher, he has over seventy scientific publications to his credit.

Anointed by God, Dr. D.K Olukoya is a prophet, evangelist, teacher and preacher of the Word. His life and that of his wife, Shade and their son, Elijah Toluwani are living proofs that all power belong to God.

The Battle Cry Christian Ministries is devoted to:

(a) Teaching and disseminating information on Christian spiritual warfare,
(b) Making available, life-changing Christian articles and books,
at affordable prices and
(c) Preparing an army of aggressive prayer warriors and intercessors in this end-time.

Published by:
The Battle Cry Christian Ministries
ISBN 978-2947-70-9

Made in the USA
Monee, IL
24 December 2024

75345272R00138